Waléria R

BibleVenture centers™

Creation—
God's Awesome Power

Group
Loveland, Colorado
www.group.com

Group resources actually work!

This Group resource helps you focus on **"The 1 Thing™"**—a life-changing relationship with Jesus Christ. "The 1 Thing" incorporates our R.E.A.L. approach to ministry. It reinforces a growing friendship with Jesus, encourages long-term learning, and results in life transformation, because it's:

Relational
Learner-to-learner interaction enhances learning and builds Christian friendships.

Experiential
What learners experience through discussion and action sticks with them up to 9 times longer than what they simply hear or read.

Applicable
The aim of Christian education is to equip learners to be both hearers and doers of God's Word.

Learner-based
Learners understand and retain more when the learning process takes into consideration how they learn best.

BibleVenture Centers™: Creation—God's Awesome Power
Copyright © 2005 Group Publishing, Inc.

Visit our Web site: **www.group.com**

Credits
Author: Debbie Gowensmith
Editor: Mikal Keefer
Chief Creative Officer: Joani Schultz
Copy Editor: Ann Jahns
Art Director/Designer: Helen H. Harrison
Print Production Artist: Joyce Douglas
Illustrator: Matt Wood
Cover Art Director/Designer: Bambi Eitel
Cover Illustrator: Patty O'Friel
Production Manager: Peggy Naylor

Library of Congress Cataloging-in-Publication Data
Creation--God's awesome power.
        p. cm. -- (BibleVenture centers)
    ISBN 0-7644-2810-1 (pbk. : alk. paper)
    1. Creationism--juvenile literature. I. Group Publishing. II. Series.
    BS651.C6925 2005
    268'.432--dc22
                                                                2005005067

10 9 8 7 6 5 4 3 2 1   14 13 12 11 10 09 08 07 06 05
Printed in the United States of America.

Contents

Welcome to Bible Ventures ™

Ever wish you could connect with *all* your kids—not just the few who seem to naturally enjoy your classroom?

Most Christian educators find themselves wondering why Nancy tracks along with the lesson while Jason is busy poking his neighbors. And why does Darrell light up when it's time to be in a drama, but he'd rather eat worms than do an art project?

If you've wondered if you're a poor teacher or you've got a roomful of aliens, relax. You're dealing with learning styles—and covering all the bases is a challenge every classroom leader faces. You're not alone.

God wired different children differently. That's a good thing—otherwise, we'd live in a world populated solely by mechanical engineers. Or maybe everyone would be an artist and our world would be a dazzling burst of color and music—but the bridges would all fall down.

We *need* to have different people in the world...and in the church.

BibleVentures gives you the opportunity for hands-on exploration of key Bible events using a variety of learning styles. You'll open up the truth of the Bible point and the Scripture passage to a wide variety of children, whether they learn best through their ears...their fingers...or their eyes. You'll engage children and provide a "wow!" of surprise as kids move from one BibleVenture Center to another.

And best of all, you'll know that you're helping long-term, high-impact learning to happen. Your kids won't just be *hearing* God's Word; they'll *experience* it. You'll plant it deep in their hearts and minds.

So get ready for a learning adventure. *You'll* know you're providing a balanced, learning experience that taps a range of learning styles, but your kids won't know...or care.

They'll just know they're having a blast learning—and that in your class, you speak their language.

How to Use This Program

Each week children will gather as one large group at **The Depot**—the launching spot for their weekly adventures. Here they'll experience a fun opening that draws their attention to the Bible Point.

From The Depot, children move with their designated group to one of the four **Venture Centers**. Children will remain in their Venture Centers for 40 minutes, and while there dive deeply into one portion of the Bible story through dramas, games, music, puppets, or other fun activities. Then everyone returns to The Depot for a time of closing and celebration.

Included in your BibleVentures **book are:**
- 1 leader's section,
- 1 set of leader job descriptions,
- 4 Venture Center Leaders sections,
- 4 reproducible take-home sheets,
- 1 reproducible CD, and
- reproducible visas.

You'll use these resources to lead children on an exciting and interactive four-week journey through the parable of the good Samaritan.

Also included for your use, should you choose to use them, are
- a sample invitation letter to help you encourage kids in your church and your neighborhood to attend,
- BibleVenture Center Leader encouragers—so your volunteers grow in their commitment to serving kids and Christ,
- a brief article to send to your leaders about how to connect with kids, and
- a teacher-training session!

Ready to get started? Here are five simple steps to take as you pull together your BibleVenture Center...

1. Recruit leaders.
You'll need five Venture Center Leaders for this BibleVenture.

One leader will oversee The Depot gatherings. The other four leaders will run the four Venture Centers, the learning centers small groups of children will visit. Review the different Venture Centers *before* recruiting leaders; that way you'll be

Bible Point Alert!

As children move through this BibleVenture program, they'll discover a foundational Bible truth—a Bible Point. The Bible Point is mentioned often in each Venture Center. Encourage your kids to explore the Bible Point, and live it out every day of the week!

able to match up the major learning style used in each center with someone who enjoys connecting with kids in that way.

For instance, if you have a center that uses lots of music, find a bouncy, fun song leader who loves Jesus and loves kids. If a center uses art to tell a Bible story, ask an artistic, crafty person to lead that center.

One plus of the BibleVenture method of teaching is that teachers get to use their strengths! But that only happens if you're careful to match centers with teachers.

The person leading The Depot will have new material to present each week, while the Venture Center Leaders will teach one session four times over the course of four weeks. Since a new group of children rotates through the center each week, the leader can use the same lesson four times!

This approach allows for less weekly preparation on the part of your center leaders. And they'll improve from week to week as they fine-tune their presentations.

You'll also need some BibleVenture Buddies.

These are adults or capable teenagers who each befriend a small group of children. We call those small groups "Venture Teams." **BibleVenture Buddies** hang out with their Venture Teams and serve as a guide, facilitator, and friend.

BibleVenture Buddies don't prepare lessons or teach. Instead, they get to know their kids. Buddies learn names, pray for the children in their Venture Teams, and reach out to kids in appropriate ways. If Jodie is absent, it's the BibleVenture Buddy who sends a postcard to let her know she was missed. If Jodie is sick, it's her BibleVenture Buddy who calls to encourage her.

BibleVenture Buddies show up for class ten minutes early so they're ready to greet children. They travel with kids to different centers each week and enthusiastically join in to play the games, do the art project, sing the music, and do whatever else the children do.

Your BibleVenture Buddies aren't teachers, but they help kids connect with the Bible truth being taught in each center. Because they get to know their kids, they're perfectly positioned to help relate the Bible truths to individual kids' lives.

How many BibleVenture Buddies will you need? It depends on how many children participate in your program. For purposes of crowd control and relationship building, it's best if Venture Teams are between five and seven children, and you'll need one BibleVenture Buddy for each group. You'll keep the same group of children together throughout your four-week adventure.

And here's a tip for leaders: Look for BibleVenture Buddies among people who *haven't* been Christian education volunteers in the past. Clearly communicate that you're not asking these folks to teach; you're asking them to be a

friend to a small group of children. This is a completely *different* job than being a Sunday school teacher!

2. Give each leader his or her section of this book.

Don't worry—those sections are reproducible for use in your local church. So is the CD, so ask a student in your congregation to burn a copy for each of the leaders. Copying CDs is easy, inexpensive, and—as long as you use the CDs in your church only—completely legal!

Here's how to distribute the pages:
- The Depot—pages 27-46
- Venture Center One—The Drama and Creative Movement Center: pages 47-60
- Venture Center Two—The Art Center: pages 61-68
- Venture Center Three—The Games Center: pages 69-76
- Venture Center Four—The Audio-Visual Center: pages 77-83

3. Create groups of children.

When you're creating individual **Venture Teams**, form your groups with children of various ages. This allows older children to help the younger ones and to be role models. It also results in fewer discipline problems.

"What?" you may be thinking. "Not keep all my third-grade girls together? They'll go on strike!"

Trust us: When you create Venture Teams that combine several ages, *especially* if you have an adult volunteer travel with each group, you'll see fewer discipline issues arise. Children may groan a bit at first, but reassure them that they'll be able to hang out with their same-age buddies before the BibleVenture starts.

Besides, when you use mixed-age groupings, you're also separating your fifth-grade boys!

Some churches choose to create multi-age groups by combining first-through third-graders, and then creating separate groups of fourth- and fifth-graders. This is also an option.

Help children remember what Venture Team they're on by assigning each group a color. Or get into the theme of this BibleVenture and ask Venture Teams to come up with theme-based names for themselves!

As you assign children to their Venture Teams, make a notation on their name tags and on their BibleVenture Visas as to which group they're in. That way when kids sign in each week at The Depot ticket window, they'll quickly remember what group to join for the remainder of the program.

Be sure each child and adult has a name tag to wear each week. Name tags allow everyone to know each other's names (instead of saying, "You, in the blue shirt.") *and* they allow leaders to know that a child has signed in for the day's events. You can make permanent name tags that kids and leaders reuse each week, or write names on self-stick labels. A quick and easy way for kids to know what group they're in is to use name tags in colors that correspond to their Venture Team. Or use white labels and write names in colorful ink that corresponds to Venture Teams.

A note: In this BibleVenture program, it's best to use adhesive-backed sticker labels; they're used in a variety of ways during The Depot meetings.

Please note: Because you have four Venture Centers going at the same time, you need to form four groupings of children to attend them. If you have four Venture Teams, it's easy—just send one group to each Venture Center. If you have more than four teams, do what you can to have an approximately even number of kids (or groups) in each of the centers. It makes life easier for center leaders if they see about the same number of kids each week.

If you have a smaller number of children—fewer than 15—participating in your program, you might consider keeping all the kids together and doing a different Venture Center each week.

4. Make copies of visas.

You'll want a visa for each child in attendance, plus extras for visitors. You'll need them the first time you meet, so run copies now and get that out of the way.

Like the CDs, you can make as many copies as you wish so long as they're used in your local church.

5. Walk through the entire BibleVenture with your volunteers.

Invite your leaders to sit down with you and talk through what they'll be doing, when they'll do it, and where they'll be serving. Many leaders like to know where they'll hold their class so they can think through the logistics of how to stage a drama or where to store supplies from week to week.

Besides, you'll want to pray with your team and thank them for loving kids and helping kids discover Bible truths. A quick meeting is one good way to do that.

That's it—five easy steps to memorable, exciting, fun learning! *BibleVentures* is easy—and it's a blast!

The Venture Verse

During this four-week adventure about creation, children will learn Genesis 1:1, which says, "In the beginning God created the heavens and the earth."

Through exploring the creation account, your children will discover that God is wise, powerful, and sustaining. You'll help your children look at the world around them through fresh, new eyes: eyes that see how God's creation reflects his character and power.

Children will learn and apply the Venture Verse through activities in The Depot and in the Venture Centers. Consider creating a poster, banner, or other visual with the Venture Verse on it to display during this BibleVenture. Having the verse up front and visible is a boost to memory!

It's important to note that what you're after isn't just that kids can recite the verse—that wouldn't take more than ten minutes and a stack of candy bar rewards.

What you want is for children to plant the truth of the words deep in their hearts and minds. You want kids to make the connection that God was the originator of all created things—including you and them—which tells us a lot about who God is.

That's a foundational truth. A truth that may run counter to what children hear on the playground, in class, and—perhaps—at home.

At BibleVentures you won't have children memorize a blizzard of Scripture passages that will be tucked in their short-term memory today and totally gone tomorrow. Instead, kids will be exposed to the meaning of the words, and the impact of the truth that God created the world out of wisdom and power, created them, and continues to care for his creation today.

If you choose to make Bible memory a larger part of your BibleVenture Center program, great. It's easy to integrate more verses into the program. But remember that when it comes to bringing about true life change, "less is more." It's far better to focus on one verse that sinks deep into how children view themselves before God than to slide a bunch of words into their heads.

The Venture Visas

Make one BibleVenture Visa for each child. Photocopy the BibleVenture Visas on pages 15-19. Place the cover on top and the pages inside in any order—children won't necessarily move through the program in the order of the visa pages. And have a visa for each child—kids *love* having their own special visas!

Make it easier for kids to know what group they're in by having the color of the construction paper cover correspond with their group's colors.

Each week, children will take their BibleVenture Visas with them to their Venture Centers. The leader will affix a sticker or stamp the visa with a stamp to show children have traveled to that activity. As kids return to The Depot for the closing, leaders will gather the visas and return them to the leader of The Depot, who'll keep them for the following week.

At the last closing, children will receive them to take home.

This visa is the property of

_____

**and secures safe transport
and admittance to each
Venture Center for the bearer.**

"In the beginning God created the heavens and the earth" (Genesis 1:1).

Venture Visa

18

The Travel Plan

Use the following chart to help you plan where children will travel each week.

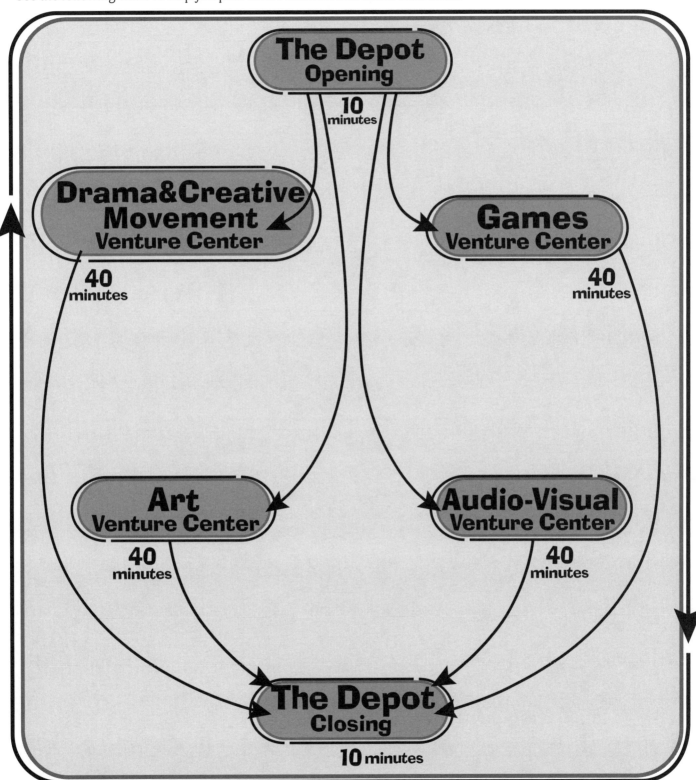

The Depot Opening

10 minutes

Drama&Creative Movement Venture Center

Games Venture Center

40 minutes

40 minutes

Art Venture Center

Audio-Visual Venture Center

40 minutes

40 minutes

The Depot Closing

10 minutes

Make the Most of Your BibleVenture

You'll be exploring God's creation of the heavens and the earth for four weeks, so make the most of it and have fun with décor and costumes. You can keep it simple with a few posters, or you can go all out and create an entire universe!

Picture your leaders wearing costumes...or the expressions of children as they enter a familiar classroom and see it's been transformed into a tropical rain forest...or their wonder as the simple tunics you've created for all the children are slipped on and cinched in place with a length of twine.

Here are some ideas to consider regarding creating a fresh, inviting BibleVenture environment:

Costumes

You and the kids can have *lots* of fun with creation-oriented costumes!

One benefit of providing costuming is that when children pull on the simple tunics you've created, cinching the tunics in place with a piece of twine or a length of cloth, they know they've entered into a different environment. They know they're at BibleVenture, and the act of putting on a costume is a transition.

An alternative to Bible-time tunics is letting children dress up as their favorite animals: Face paint can provide whiskers and noses, oven mitts become paws, and headbands can sport construction-paper ears.

For an easy-make, quick-wear animal body, cut a hole from the bottom of a paper grocery bag for a child's head, and cut armholes from the sides of the bag. Use paint or markers to decorate the sack with scales or fur. This is quick, fun, and pulls on over clothing easily.

For other accessories, shop first at thrift stores or secondhand shops. You can find animal-themed props and clothing you can easily adapt.

Keep in mind that for the purposes of your dramas, you only need one definitive prop to establish a character. For instance, while you can put a costume on the Adam character, you need only hand the child playing Adam a necktie, and that will remind everyone who's playing the part of Adam.

So don't fear simple costuming—simple is good!

But if you're the happy owner of a costume closet, or if you have sufficient time and resources to turn dramas into mini-productions, here are some costuming suggestions:

For an easy-make, quick-wear tunic, fold a length of fabric (buy cotton or muslin in quantity) in half, and cut a half circle from the fold to make an opening for the head. Use a piece of rope or thin length of fabric as a belt.

● Martha

This is a character who could benefit from a big wig and some jewelry. Be sure she's holding a wooden- or serving-spoon "microphone," too.

● Light

How to portray light? How about a yellow cloth wrapped around a child, or a bright yellow or white headband?

● Sky

A sheet of blue paper suggests open, clear skies.

● Plants and Flowers

A few plastic flowers tucked behind an ear, or held in hands, portray plants and flowers.

● The Sun, Moon, and Stars

Cut a sheet of yellow paper in a circle, a sheet of white paper in a circle, and some star shapes from white paper.

● Fish, Birds, Animals, and People

The simplest way to communicate these roles is probably how the children move.

Scenery

Consider giving your four sessions an extra bit of fun by creating a set in the room where you'll have The Depot segments of your program. Your stage or room could reflect the universe or the Garden of Eden.

If you keep the set general in nature—such as a jungle or forest set—then you can probably use it for your dramas, too.

You can create a set by...

● painting on large sheets of paper to make backdrops, then hanging them on the walls.

● drooping vines, branches, and leaves around the room. Twist rolls of brown and green construction paper and tape on green leaves. Add flowers—plastic, real, or construction-paper—for splashes of color.

● making tree trunks with heavy paper, paper rolls, or cardboard. Paint the tree

trunks brown, and sponge-paint with darker brown and black to create the texture of bark.

● placing potted plants and flowers around the space, then adding stuffed animals and cutouts of animal pictures in the trees, bushes, and vines.

● placing a swath of blue plastic wrap around one area to make a river or pond. Add stones to one side, and place toy frogs or turtles on the stones.

● creating a large sun by hanging a stuffed, bright yellow pillowcase in a corner. Use duct tape to secure yellow, orange, and red streamers to the pillowcase to represent beams of light.

● replicating the Garden of Eden at night with white Christmas lights attached to the ceiling.

The Daily Challenge™

Take advantage of the Daily Challenges™ presented in each session! These are simple, easy-to-do activities that provide children with practical ways to apply to their daily lives what they've learned at your BibleVenture.

Draw attention to the Daily Challenge to encourage children to act on what they learn at BibleVenture meetings. It's this application of Bible truth that turns interesting lessons into deep, life-changing learning. When kids *apply* Bible truth, they hide God's Word deep in their hearts.

Look for the logo you'll see in the margin each week—that's where you'll find a Daily Challenge for your children...and for yourself!

The Depot

For the next four weeks, you'll lead The Depot portion of our BibleVentures program. Each week, children will gather at The Depot for an opening time and a closing time. Each segment lasts about 10 minutes.

At The Depot, kids sing, review the Venture Verse, and participate in an attention-grabbing experience that introduces the Bible Point. The following lessons will provide all the information you need to have a great time leading this segment of the BibleVenture program!

After the opening, groups of children (Venture Teams) will travel to Venture Centers. Groups of children will stay in the Venture Centers for 40 minutes, then return to The Depot for a time of closing and celebration.

During this BibleVenture, children will explore God's creation of the world. Children will discover that God's creation shows us his glory. That's an important lesson to learn...and to remember every time they see what God made.

You'll see the "God's creation shows us his glory" Bible Point mentioned several times in your lessons. That's intentional: Repetition helps children hear and remember. And by the end of this BibleVenture program, children will have considered how wonderful God is—how wise, loving, and powerful—to have created such a world.

You've been carefully selected to serve in this role. You've got the abilities, attitude, and love of Jesus and kids that it takes to engage and involve children. You'll make good use of those abilities in this program!

Here's a quick outline of your responsibilities as leader of The Depot:

1. Meet and greet kids.

You're the upfront face kids will see each week; it matters how you go out of your way to individually greet as many children as possible. A smile and handshake or pat on the back from you can make a child's day. Because you'll be making the first impression, it's important that you arrive *before* children do.

2. Oversee visa distribution.

As children arrive at The Depot, they'll stop at the Depot ticket window to sign in, get their name tags, and pick up their BibleVenture Visas. The ticket window can be as simple as a table with a sign on it or as elaborate as a booth with a ticket window cut in it.

For an inexpensive, portable booth, set a refrigerator box on end, cut a door in the back, and cut a ticket window in the front. Prime and paint the booth

with bright colors, and you'll have a lightweight booth with room inside for one medium-sized adult.

And while you should oversee this function, it's going to be very difficult for you to staff it and take care of everything else that's happening as you lead the program. There will always be children who come a little late and want to sign in while you're up front leading a song.

So unless you can be two places at once, it's important for you to recruit a helper. We call that person the "Servant Leader" because he or she serves you and others—and that's true leadership!

You'll find a job description for the role of Servant Leader on page 89.

3. Set up for the opening—and closing!

The following lessons will tell you everything you need to know. And though the required supplies are simple and easy to find, it will help if you plan ahead.

Again—your life will be far easier if you recruit a Servant Leader to keep the supply cabinet stocked and the sign-in and sign-out processes organized.

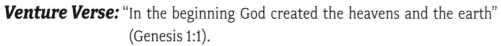

God's creation shows us his glory

Venture Verse: "In the beginning God created the heavens and the earth" (Genesis 1:1).

Supplies for Week 1

- Bible
- CD player
- *BibleVentures: Creation* CD
- flashlight with a bright light
- glow sticks or small flashlights
- pens or pencils

The Depot: *Opening*

Welcome children and encourage them to sit with their Venture Teams. SAY **It's so exciting to begin our journey together here at The Depot! We'll gather here at the beginning and end of each adventure. Since this is the first week of our adventure, I want to be sure you all know what Venture Team you'll be on for this BibleVenture.**

Have each child check his or her name tag, BibleVenture Visa, or other list you've created so children know what Venture Teams they're on. Ask children to sit with their Venture Teams during The Depot.

SAY **We're going to spend the next four weeks learning about an amazing event—the first thing that ever happened in the world! We're going to learn about creation, and creation is when God made the world.**

Open your Bible to Genesis 1:1, and hold up your Bible to show children that you're reading from the very first page.

SAY **The very first thing the Bible tells us is this: "In the beginning God created the heavens and the earth" (Genesis 1:1). Let's think about what this verse means.**

Assign each Venture Team one of the following words: *beginning, created, heavens, earth.*

Venture view

Establish a nonverbal signal to use to direct kids' attention back to yourself. Suggestion: Clap your hands, flick the lights, blow on a wooden train whistle, or use some other unusual sound maker that won't be mistaken in the midst of discussion. Practice the signal several times until kids recognize it and respond to it.

Select a flashlight for this activity that puts out a strong, bright light. If you have an intense light such as a spotlight, all the better. Before The Depot, ensure that your light has strong batteries and a functional bulb and works well.

SAY **With your BibleVenture Buddy, talk about what your word means, and create a motion or action that helps you remember the meaning of this word.**

Allow a couple of minutes for children to work in their Venture Teams, then ask BibleVenture Buddies to help their groups share their actions with the larger group. Finally, lead everyone in saying the verse together, doing the actions along with the verse.

SAY **During this BibleVenture, we'll be learning what it means that God created, or made, the heavens and the earth. Each week you'll have the chance to learn something new about God's creation as you travel to a different Venture Center. All our adventures will remind us that God created the world. In fact, (BP) God's creation shows us his glory.**

What do you think of when you hear the word _glory_?

Shine a bright flashlight at a few kids whose hands are raised so they can share their ideas with the whole group. Then have children discuss the meaning of the word _glory_ with their Venture Teams.

After a minute or two, get everyone's attention again. Turn off the lights, and shine the bright flashlight around the room as you speak.

SAY **Some people say glory is like a pure, bright light—a light so perfect and strong that nothing can put it out or make it even the tiniest bit darker. God is so perfect and strong that nothing can make his goodness fail or shrink. Only our perfect and strong God could make this wonderful world. (BP) God's creation shows us his glory.**

Explain that you're going to shine the beam of light on different people or groups of people. When the light rests on them, they should shout out, (BP) "God's creation shows us his glory!"

When everyone understands, shine the light around the crowd, resting the beam on different groups of people so they can shout out the Bible Point.

SAY **God made a beautiful, amazing world. Everything God created—all the heavens and the earth—shows us that God is powerful and wise and loving. Let's sing praises to tell God that we appreciate how great he is.**

Lead children in singing "Hymn of Praise" (track 10 on the _BibleVentures: Creation_ CD).

SAY **God is great, and we can remember just how great God is every time we see what he created. While you're at your Venture Centers today, think about how (BP) God's creation shows us his glory. Now it's time to travel to your Venture Centers!**

The lyrics to the songs on your _BibleVentures: Creation_ CD are on pages 84-86 of this manual.

Have the leaders of each Venture Center guide the Venture Teams to the area where they'll be meeting. Children will remain at the Venture Centers for 40 minutes. When 35 minutes have passed, signal the Venture Center Leaders to let them know it's time to wrap up their activities and move children back to The Depot for the closing.

The Depot: *Closing*

Turn off the lights in the room before the closing. As children enter, distribute glow sticks or flashlights—one for each child if you have enough or one per team if you don't—so kids can find their way to their seats. Also start singing "He's Got the Whole World in His Hands" (track 11 on the CD), and continue singing until all the Venture Teams have returned to The Depot.

Hold a flashlight, and shine it on your own face.

SAY **Welcome back to The Depot! I'm sure each of you had an exciting adventure as you learned more about God's creation of the heavens and the earth. As we learn about God's creation, we want to remember that (BP) God's creation shows us his glory. Let's think about how great it is to have a glorious God watching over us.**

Explain that you're going to ask a question and that anyone who wants to answer should hold a light up high. When you see the light, you'll shine your flashlight on the child so he or she can answer.

ASK

● **What did the flashlight do for you today?**

● **What does the sun do for us? What about the moon and stars?**

Use your flashlight to select different children to answer the questions.

SAY **One reason God gave us lights like the sun, the moon, and the stars was to help us find our way in the darkness. God's glory is like that too. Because God is so wise and powerful and loving, he can show us the way. We can follow God just as you followed the lights into the room.**

(BP) **God's creation shows us his glory. God made the sun, the moon, and the stars. They can remind us that we can follow our glorious God.**

ASK

● **How can you follow God this week?**

Again, use your flashlight to select different children to answer the question. Afterward, turn on the lights.

If you'd like to extend your time of worship and singing, lead children in singing one or more of the other songs on the *BibleVentures: Creation* CD.

You can find glow sticks—those plastic sticks that light up when you shake them—at many craft, party, or discount stores. If you can't find glow sticks, you often can find small, inexpensive flashlights at the same types of stores.

If you can't gather together enough glow sticks or flashlights for all your children, ask BibleVenture Buddies to act as "ushers." Give each Buddy a flashlight, and have him or her lead children to their seats one small group at a time.

Be sure to call on as many different children as possible. One child is sure to have his or her hand up over and over. Encourage this child to save that idea until all the other children have had a chance to share too.

SAY **You've come up with some really great ideas! Now I'd like each of you to silently decide on one of these ideas, and write that idea on the inside cover of your Venture Visa. For example, you might write, "I will follow God by reading my Bible." Or you might say, "I'll follow God by being nice to my sister." Or if you'd rather draw a picture of that idea, that's great too!**

Your BibleVenture Buddy will be looking at what you write or draw in order to pray for you this week.

Ask BibleVenture Buddies to help distribute pens or pencils to the children, and encourage older children to help younger ones who may not be confident in their writing skills.

Allow a few minutes for children to write or draw in their visas. When children have finished, have them hold their Venture Visas in their hands and bow their heads for prayer.

PRAY **Dear God, thank you for creating such a wonderful world. Help us to think of your glory when we see all the great things you've created. Your creation shows us that you are wise, powerful, and loving. It reminds us that we can follow you. As we hold our Venture Visas, we ask that you'll use your power to help us do the actions we've written inside. We praise you because you are a wise, powerful, and loving God. In Jesus' name, amen.**

Ask children to leave their Venture Visas (and name tags if you've created permanent ones) at the ticket window as they leave. Turn on the CD, and let those children still waiting for their parents join you in singing a few more songs of praise.

The Depot

God's creation shows us his glory **BP**

Venture Verse: "In the beginning God created the heavens and the earth" (Genesis 1:1).

Supplies for Week 2

- CD player
- *BibleVentures: Creation* CD
- chair
- balls of yarn
- watch with a second hand
- scissors

The Depot: *Opening*

Welcome children and encourage them to sit with their Venture Teams. Be sure that children who were not here last week know which Venture Team to join and are welcomed warmly.

SAY **We're back to continue our BibleVenture about God's creation. God made an amazing heaven and earth, and BP God's creation shows us his glory.**

You know, people are always trying to figure out *how* God made the heavens and the earth. Scientists all over the world study that, but they're never really sure how it happened. God is smarter than any scientist in the world—way smarter.

Scientists also are studying how our own bodies work. They are very hard to figure out, but our bodies do amazing things.

Just think about *one* amazing thing our bodies have: reflexes. A reflex is when our body moves without us even thinking about it. For example, if you touch a hot stove, your hand jerks back right away. You didn't have to take the time to think, "Oh my, that's very hot. I think I should move my hand away from that stove now."

How many of you have had a reflex test at the doctor's office? Pause for kids to raise their hands.

If you have a large group—too large for one ball of yarn—then create three or four different groups before beginning this activity. Have a volunteer for each team come to the front of the room to start off and receive the "message." Be sure someone times how long each group's message takes to make the rounds.

This is when the doctor hits your knee with a tiny hammer to see if your leg will move. Scientists have figured out that your knee sends a message all the way through your body to your brain. There, your brain recognizes the signal and sends a message down to your leg, telling it to move. God created this amazing system to be super fast. It takes less than one second!

Let's try the reflex test to see how fast God created our reflexes to be.

Ask a child to volunteer to demonstrate the reflex test. Have him or her join you at the front and sit with legs dangling from a chair. Use the edge of your hand to gently strike the soft part of the knee—just below the kneecap. Try a few times to see if you can get the volunteer's leg to jump. Then encourage children to work with partners to do the reflex test, using only their hands—no hammers!

After a minute, use your attention-getter to return everyone's attention to yourself.

SAY **Now let's compare God's reflex system to our own system of getting a message out and back.**

Hold up a large ball of yarn, and explain that it represents the message the brain is sending. Tell children you're going to time how long it takes to get the message to everyone in the group and then back to you.

Wrap a loop of yarn around your wrist as you repeat the Bible Point. Then note the time on a watch while you hand the ball of yarn to someone close to you. Have him or her repeat the Bible Point while wrapping a loop of yarn around his or her wrist and then passing the ball of yarn to the next person. Repeat until everyone has said the Bible Point and looped the yarn around his or her wrist.

When the yarn reaches you again, call out how much time the activity took.

SAY **Somehow God figured out how to make our reflex system so that it takes less than a second to get a message to the brain and back. This is just one example of how**  **God's creation shows us his glory. It took us** [time] **to get a message from me to you and back.**

Have children remove the yarn from their wrists. Ask BibleVenture Buddies to form their kids into groups of three to discuss the following questions.

ASK

● **What amazing things do you know about God's creation?**

● **What does the way God made us tell you about him?**

As children are talking, pull all the yarn back toward yourself again and set it aside.

SAY **God made our bodies in an amazing way! Let's praise God for his wonderful creation.**

Lead children in singing "I Sing the Mighty Power of God" (track 12) on the CD.

SAY **God created the heavens and the earth, so we know that God is creative and powerful—more powerful than anybody in the world. God knows the way everything works. As you're at your Venture Centers today, think about how (BP) God's creation shows us his glory. It's now time to travel to your Venture Centers!**

Have BibleVenture Buddies guide their Venture Teams to the Venture Centers assigned to them. Children will remain at the Venture Centers for 40 minutes. When 35 minutes have passed, signal the Venture Center Leaders to let them know it's time to wrap up their activities and move children back to The Depot for the closing.

The Depot: *Closing*

As children begin entering the room, start singing "He's Got the Whole World in His Hands" (track 11 on the CD). Continue singing until all the groups have returned to The Depot.

SAY **Welcome back to The Depot! I'm sure each of you had an exciting adventure as you learned more about God's creation of the heavens and the earth. As we learn about God's creation, we want to remember that (BP) God's creation shows us his glory!**

Ask children to take out their Venture Visas and sit in a circle with their Venture Teams. Ask children to review with their BibleVenture Buddies what kids wrote on the inside cover last week. Remind kids that they wrote one way they could follow God last week. Ask several children who did the actions they wrote inside their Venture Visas to share what they did and what happened.

SAY **Does anyone remember our Venture Verse? Our verse is Genesis 1:1, and it says, "In the beginning God created the heavens and the earth." God created the world, including you and me, so he can help us with anything! If you didn't do the action you wrote last week, you can pray and ask God to help you do it this week.**

Let's think more about what it means that God created you and me.

Ask BibleVenture Buddies to come forward and collect a piece of yarn for each child in his or her Venture Team. Have Buddies distribute the yarn pieces,

If you'd like to extend your time of worship and singing, lead children in singing one or more of the other songs on the *BibleVentures: Creation* CD.

Before children arrive, cut the yarn into 4- to 6-inch pieces. You'll want one piece for each child.

giving one to each child. Then have kids form pairs, and encourage younger children to partner with older children. Ask BibleVenture Buddies to help the kids pair up.

SAY **Each person should create a shape from your piece of yarn. You might tie your yarn into a circle or place it on the floor in the shape of a cross—or any other shape you choose.**

Give kids a few seconds to create their shapes. Then have one child in each pair close his or her eyes and describe the shape he or she created to the partner. Afterward, have kids switch roles.

ASK

● **How well did you remember the shape of your yarn? Why did you remember the shape as well as you did?**

SAY **That wasn't hard at all, was it? You created the shape, so of course you knew everything about it.**

Well, God knows his creation just as well because *he* **created the heavens and the earth. The book of Job in the Bible says God knows when the animals have their babies, where the winds go, what the weather is like all around the world, and how the sun shines. Because God made the world, he knows everything about it. God even knows all about the shape you just created! That's why 🅱🅿 God's creation shows us his glory.**

When we see the things God created, we can remember God's glory and how powerful and loving God is.

Have pairs discuss the following questions.

ASK

● **How do you feel when you think about the fact that God knows everything about the world?**

● **What in your life makes you feel unsure or afraid?**

● **How do you think God can help you with those scary things?**

SAY **Hold your yarn shape in your hand. Just as you created that yarn shape, God created you and knows all about you. God even knows what makes you feel unsure or afraid. That's why we can trust that God is powerful enough to help us with any trouble we face.**

Tell kids to place their pieces of yarn inside their Venture Visas as reminders that God knows them better than anyone and can help them with any troubles they face.

PRAY **Dear God, help us to remember this week how powerful and glorious you are when we see what you've created.**

When we're afraid or unsure, help us to remember that you understand everything about the world—including everything about us. We are amazed by how wonderful you are! Please help us when we're unsure or afraid. Thank you. In Jesus' name, amen.

Ask children to leave their Venture Visas (and name tags if you've created permanent ones) at the ticket window as they leave. Play the CD and let those children still waiting for their parents join you in singing a few more songs of praise.

Make life easy for your BibleVenture Buddies and yourself by making a copy of the questions for each leader. Then you won't have to keep interrupting the discussion flow to ask the next question.

God's creation shows us his glory

Venture Verse: "In the beginning God created the heavens and the earth" (Genesis 1:1).

Supplies for Week 3
- CD player
- *BibleVentures: Creation* CD
- chairs
- clay
- large, metal paper clips
- balloons
- pens or pencils

The Depot: *Opening*

Welcome children and encourage them to sit with their Venture Teams. Be sure that children who were not here last week know which Venture Team to join and are welcomed warmly.

SAY **We're back to continue our BibleVenture about God's creation. God made an amazing heaven and earth, and**  **God's creation shows us his glory.**

Each time we meet, you're hearing about God's incredible creation. Do you remember the Venture Verse from Genesis 1:1?

Lead children in saying the verse together: **"In the beginning God created the heavens and the earth."** You're also learning that creation shows us that **God is the most amazing being in the whole universe: Nothing and no one is wiser, more loving, or more powerful.**

Part of what makes God glorious is his amazing power—and we can see a little bit of that power by seeing what God made. Let's think about what it means to have power.

Ask BibleVenture Buddies to help the kids in their groups form pairs. In each

Venture view

The "powerful index finger" activity won't work unless kids are seated on chairs. If kids are sitting on the floor, skip this activity and move on to the next one.

pair, one child should sit on a chair with his or her back against the backrest. The other child should stand facing his or her seated partner.

SAY **To those of you who are standing up, you have an amazing amount of power. You have so much power that you can keep your partner seated with only your index finger!**

First, to those of you who are seated, there are a couple of rules: You may not lean forward, and you may not use your arms.

Now to those of you who are standing up, place your index finger on your partner's forehead. You don't need to press hard because that one finger has a lot of power!

Now those of you who are seated, please try to stand up without leaning forward and without using your hands.

If the seated partners follow the rules, they will not be able to stand up. The body needs to lean forward in order to shift the center of gravity enough to stand. Allow kids to switch roles and try again.

SAY **I have another test to show how powerful you are.**

Have children stay in their pairs and move to the walls of the room. Explain that one partner should stand with his or her back and heels against the wall. Have the other partners use their super-powerful index fingers to point to a spot on the floor just in front of where their partners are standing.

SAY **For those of you standing against the wall, there are a couple of rules again: You may not bend your knees, and you may not move your feet. The pointers' index fingers are so powerful that they can prevent you from touching the spot on the floor.**

Challenge the kids who are standing with their backs against the walls to touch the spots on the floor that their partners are pointing to. If they follow the rules, they won't be able to; they'd fall over first! Allow kids to switch roles, and then ask them to return to their seats.

SAY **Of course, there are good reasons why you couldn't stand up or bend over in these experiments. And it's *not* that our index fingers are so amazingly powerful!**

In fact, the reason has to do with God's power again.

God created a powerful system called gravity, and you couldn't stand up because of that system. You couldn't touch the spot on the floor because of that powerful system. **BP** **God's creation shows us his glory. When we experience**

gravity, we can remember how powerful God is. Let's celebrate God's mighty power!

If you'd like to extend your time of worship and singing, lead children in singing one or more of the other songs on the *BibleVentures: Creation* CD.

Lead the children in singing "I Sing the Mighty Power of God" (track 12) on the CD.

SAY **God created the heavens and the earth, so we know God is more powerful than anybody or anything in the world. As you're at your Venture Centers today, think about how** **BP** **God's creation shows us his glory. It's now time to travel to your Venture Centers!**

Have BibleVenture Buddies guide their Venture Teams to the Venture Centers assigned to them. Children will remain at the Venture Centers for 40 minutes. When 35 minutes have passed, signal the Venture Center Leaders to let them know it's time to wrap up their activities and move children back to The Depot for the closing.

The Depot: *Closing*

As children enter the room, start singing "What a Mighty God We Serve" (track 13 on the CD). Continue singing until all the Venture Teams have returned to The Depot and everyone is singing with you.

SAY **Welcome back to The Depot! I'm sure each of you had an exciting adventure as you learned more about God's creation of the heavens and the earth. As we learn about God's creation, we want to remember that** **BP** **God's creation shows us God's glory!**

We were just singing about the power of God, which we can remember every time we see God's creation. Let's think more about God's mighty power.

Have BibleVenture Buddies help their Venture Team form pairs or trios. Then ask Buddies to help you distribute to each group a lump of clay about the size of a Ping-Pong ball, a large metal paper clip, and a balloon. Have older kids blow up and tie off balloons, and encourage BibleVenture Buddies and older children to help those who are having problems with this.

Explain that one child should form the piece of clay into a ball. Another child should push the paper clip into the ball of clay so that the clip stands straight up. The third child should rub the balloon on his or her hair and then hold the balloon close to the paper clip—*without* touching it. A small spark will shoot between the clip and the balloon. Ask BibleVenture Buddies to circulate among their Venture Team members to provide assistance as needed.

After a few minutes, get children's attention again.

Make life easy for your BibleVenture Buddies and yourself by making a copy of the questions for each leader. Then you won't have to keep interrupting the discussion flow to ask the next question.

SAY **Our experiment made a tiny amount of power, a small spark. God's power made the heavens and the earth! Nothing is more powerful than God, and God's creation reminds us of that.** **BP** **God's creation shows us his glory.**

Select volunteers to collect the balloons, clay, and paper clips and set them at the front of the room. Meanwhile, lead children in singing, "I Sing the Mighty Power of God" (track 12 on the CD). Every time you sing the word *mighty*, lead children in curling their biceps to make muscles; every time you sing the word *God*, lead children in pointing toward the sky.

Ask children to sit in a circle with their Venture Teams to discuss the following questions.

ASK

● **How do you feel knowing that the God who loves you is so powerful?**

● **How have you seen or felt God's power in your life?**

● **What troubles are in your life right now?**

● **How can God's power help you with those troubles?**

PRAY **God, help us to remember this week how powerful you are when we see what you've created. When we have troubles in our lives, help us to remember that you are more powerful than anyone or anything. With your love and power, please help us with the troubles we face. Thank you. In Jesus' name, amen.**

God's creation shows us his glory

Venture Verse: "In the beginning God created the heavens and the earth" (Genesis 1:1).

Supplies for Week 4

- CD player
- *BibleVentures: Creation* CD
- sack filled with grocery items
- four gift boxes, wrapped (Inside the first box, place an item of food such as apples; in the second box, place a bottle of water; in the third box, place a picture of the sun; in the fourth box, place nothing.)

The Depot: *Opening*

Welcome children and encourage them to sit with their Venture Teams. Be sure that children who were not here last week know which Venture Team to join and are welcomed warmly.

SAY **We're back to continue our BibleVenture about God's creation. God made an amazing heaven and earth, and** **God's creation shows us his glory. Does anyone remember our Venture Verse, Genesis 1:1? Let's say it together.**

Lead kids in saying, "In the beginning God created the heavens and the earth."

SAY **What things have you noticed today that God created?** Have kids shout out answers. **Is there anything in this room that God created? If you see something that you think God created, point to it.** Pause for kids to respond.

God's creation really is all around us—probably more than we even realize. With all those things God created, he's given us everything we need to live. Everything and more! Let's look at some of the things God created for us.

Set out a sack filled with grocery items: milk, eggs, a can of soup, bread, apples, a newspaper, a dish towel, and so on. Have a member or two from each

If you'd like to extend your time of worship and singing, lead children in singing one or more of the other songs on the *BibleVentures: Creation* CD.

Venture Team come to the front of the room and take an item back to their Venture Team.

Explain that the BibleVenture Buddies should lead their group members in figuring out what from God's creation went into their items, including any packaging.

For example, for bread, kids might name wheat plants, sugar from sugar cane or honey from bees, oil from plants, yeast (a naturally occurring fungus-like creation), and milk from cows. They might also know that the paper or plastic bag covering the bread comes from trees or petroleum (which naturally develops from decayed plants under the right conditions), respectively.

For a can of soup, kids might name the various plants that gave the vegetables and any animals that gave meat, in addition to the naturally occurring mineral (cassiterite) from which we make tin containers.

For a carton of milk, kids might name the cows that gave the milk, the tree that gave the paper, and the bees and honey or the plants that gave the wax (often used to coat paper milk cartons or even fruit).

Give groups a couple of minutes to work, and then have each group report what they found to the larger group. Then have volunteers return the grocery items to the front and return to their seats. Thank them for their help.

SAY **We can see how much God loves us just by looking at what he created. Isn't it cool that** 🔵 **God's creation shows us his glory?**

All these things God created are blessings to us. Blessings are like gifts. God loves us so much that he blessed us with everything we need to live. He also blessed us with fun extras like beautiful colors, amazing sounds, and tasty foods! Let's sing about God's blessings to us.

💿 Lead children in singing "His Blessings Go Rolling Along" (track 14 on the *BibleVenture: Creation* CD).

SAY **God loves us so much that he blessed us with everything we need to live. We only have to look at God's creation to see how much he loves us.**

Today is your last adventure in learning about God's creation. As you're at your Venture Center today, think about how 🔵 **God's creation shows us his glory. It's now time to travel to your Venture Centers!**

Have BibleVenture Buddies guide their Venture Teams to the Venture Centers assigned to them. Children will remain at the Venture Centers for 40 minutes. When 35 minutes have passed, signal the Venture Center Leaders to let them know it's time to wrap up their activities and move children back to The Depot for the closing.

The Depot: *Closing*

As children enter the room, start singing "His Blessings Go Rolling Along" (track 14 on the CD). Continue singing until all the Venture Teams have returned to The Depot and are singing with you.

SAY **Welcome back to The Depot! I'm sure each of you had an exciting adventure as you learned more about God's creation of the heavens and the earth. And as we learn about God's creation, we want to remember that** **BP** **God's creation shows us his glory!**

When we see what God has created, we can remember how much he loves us. God has blessed us with everything we need to live. What a wonderful gift!

Before children arrive, place the four gift-wrapped boxes under the seats children will occupy. You'll want each Venture Team to find a gift box in its area.

Explain that each Venture Team should be able to find a gift box near its seats. Ask groups to find the boxes but not to open them yet. When each group has found a box, ask one group to open its box, pass it around to all the Venture Team members, and shout out what's inside. Repeat this process until all Venture Teams have revealed what is inside their boxes. Translate the discoveries to the entire group as "food," "water," "sun," and "air."

SAY **Without God's creation, we wouldn't be able to live. We need the sun to grow, the air to breathe, clean water to drink, and food to eat. God has given us these things. Let's think about what these gifts mean to us.**

Ask BibleVenture Buddies to form their kids into groups of two or three to discuss the following questions.

ASK

● **How was opening that box like receiving the gift of God's creation?**

● **How do you use the gift of God's creation every day?**

● **What does it mean to you that the world was a gift created by God?**

● **How do you think we should treat God's gifts to us?**

● **How do you think we should treat God's creation?**

SAY **BP** **God's creation shows us his glory. That means that when we see what God has created, we can remember that he is wise, powerful, and loving. We can remember that God loved us enough to give us everything we need to live. Through creation, God takes care of us.**

God's world is a special gift, and we should take care of it, too. Let's sing a song as a prayer of praise to God for the gift of creation.

Make life easy for your BibleVenture Buddies and yourself by making a copy of the questions for each leader. Then you won't have to keep interrupting the discussion flow to ask the next question.

Lead children in singing "Doxology" (track 15 on the *BibleVentures: Creation* CD).

SAY **As you leave today, take your Venture Visa with you. This booklet will be a reminder of the travels you've had in this BibleVenture on God's creation. And it can remind you that** (BP) **God's creation shows us his glory! When you see God's creation, you can think about how wise, powerful, and loving our God is.**

Continue playing songs from the CD as children leave, and let those children still waiting for their parents join you in singing a few more songs of praise.

Alternate Opening or Closing for The Depot

If one of the activities for the opening or closing in The Depot won't work for your setting or facility, you can substitute these ideas:

● Lead your children on a walk outside, or distribute old magazines for children to look through. Have children identify things that God created and share what those items tell them about God. For example, a child may point out a tree that offers cool shade, which helps the child remember that God cares for us.

● Provide children with small paper cups, soil, bean seeds, and water. Allow kids to plant their seeds in the cups and add a little water. Encourage kids to take their seeds home and watch them grow as a reminder of God's wisdom, power, and love.

Venture Center One:

God's creation shows us his glory

Venture Verse: "In the beginning God created the heavens and the earth" (Genesis 1:1).

Welcome!

You'll be leading the Drama and Creative Movement Venture Center for the next four weeks. One great piece of news is that preparing for the four weeks is easy because you prepare just *one* week's lesson—and present it four times!

Here's how your Venture Center works: Each week children gather at The Depot for a time of opening and adventure. While at The Depot, children will get together in their Venture Teams, and then one group (it could be one Venture Team or several, but each will have an adult leader) will travel to your Venture Center. This group of children will stay with you for 40 minutes, then return to The Depot for a time of closing and celebration.

In the weeks that follow, different groups of children will come to your Venture Center. You'll repeat the same activity for all four weeks, each week with a different group of children. This allows you to prepare just once and have four weeks of meaningful interaction with children as you lead them closer to God!

Your Venture Center

During this BibleVenture, children will learn about God's creation. Children will discover that God's creation shows us his glory.

You'll notice that the Bible Point, "God's creation shows us his glory," is mentioned several times in your lesson. That's by intent, and it's important that you reinforce the point by saying it each time—or even more often. By the end of this BibleVenture, children will have considered what it means that God's creation reveals his glory—his wisdom, power, and love.

In your Venture Center, children will use drama and creative movement to explore God's creation. There's no memorizing lines or turning script pages; children either listen to sections of the CD as directed in the lesson, acting along with the CD, or move their bodies to your instructions. Some of the roles require

more action and participation than others, but it's important for *every* child to have an opportunity to participate.

Children also will dig into the Venture Verse for this unit: "In the beginning God created the heavens and the earth" (Genesis 1:1). Kids will perform dramas and try to mimic each other's creative actions. Between the activities, you'll lead children in several discussion sessions.

Your enthusiasm for this Venture Center and the activities will be passed on to the children you meet each week. Greet them with excitement, encourage them to join in, and have fun!

Preparation

Before children arrive, gather these supplies:
- Bible
- CD player
- *BibleVentures: Creation* CD
- a stamp or small stickers to mark in visas (a thumbs up, if you can find it)
- a pretend microphone, such as a wooden spoon or metal serving spoon
- flashlight with a strong light
- flower lei (plastic is acceptable)
- necktie
- pens or pencils
- animal costumes, such as ears and paws, and plant costumes, such as plastic flowers woven through hair and clothes (For more costume ideas, see the leader's manual for The Depot.)

If you like, videotape one of the dramas or other activities. Kids won't have time to watch themselves performing each activity during the Venture Center, but you may have time to show them the drama before they return to The Depot.

The script that matches what you'll hear on the CD is included in this leader guide, beginning on page 55. You will *not* need to provide this for the children, as there are not parts to read or memorize. The script is provided for your reference. Listen to the CD one time before your first meeting so you're familiar with the drama.

Designate a stage area in the room where you'll meet. This may be one side of the room or an actual stage. If some children do not wish to participate, they may sit in your audience. However, try to encourage everyone to participate; since most kids will be acting in a troupe, shy children won't have to endure individual attention.

The Venture Center

As children enter, warmly welcome them to your Venture Center.

SAY **We're going to enjoy a great adventure together learning about God's creation through drama and movement! Everyone will have lots of chances to join in. We're going to put on two plays and do other fun things.**

Let's start with acting out a play. This play is about the very beginning of the Bible.

Open your Bible to Genesis 1:1, and show the page to the kids.

SAY **Genesis 1:1 is the very first sentence in the Bible. It says, "In the beginning God created the heavens and the earth."**

Have kids repeat the verse with you.

SAY **In this play about the beginning of the world, the parts are all easy to follow since there are no lines to read or memorize. You'll hear what you're supposed to do as I play the CD. Listen carefully, and just do the appropriate actions. Let's get going!**

Point out the room's stage area. Choose someone to play "Martha" and someone to play "God." Martha should stand to one side of the stage area holding a "microphone." If possible, the child playing "God" should stand off the stage area, where he or she can't be seen well. Shine a light onto the stage area whenever "God" speaks on the CD.

The rest of the children will play a drama team. Have them stand across the front of the stage area with room between each child. Explain that they'll simply act out what the voices on the CD say to do. Allow children a couple of minutes to put on costumes, if they wish.

When the kids understand their parts and are ready to go, explain that the scene begins with an announcer's voice introducing Martha, who then introduces "God."

 play "A Good Thing" (track 1). Stop the CD after the segment ends.

SAY **You did a great job! The events that the character playing God described in this play were written down in the first chapter of the first book of the Bible: Genesis 1.**

Ask children to circle up with their Venture Buddy and discuss:

● **What do you think was the most amazing thing God did when he created the heavens and the earth?**

Allow a minute or two for discussion, then use your attention-getter to draw attention back to yourself. Ask BibleVenture Buddies to each report one interesting thing mentioned in their group.

Establish a nonverbal signal to use to direct kids' attention back to yourself. Suggestion: Clap your hands, flick the lights, blow on a wooden train whistle, or use another unusual sound maker that won't be mistaken in the midst of discussion. Practice the signal several times until kids recognize it and respond to it.

To see the beam of light representing God during these dramas, dim the lights a bit or close window coverings. The room doesn't need to be dark—just dim enough to register the beam of light.

If you don't have a bright light or a room you can dim, have the child playing "God" blow soap bubbles from offstage whenever God speaks.

Then explain that you're going to move along to a second act of your drama.

Choose a different "Martha" and "God," and make sure they have their respective props. Explain that during this portion of the drama, actors will have specific roles to play. Select approximately an equal number of actors to portray each of these roles: light, sky, plants and flowers, the sun and moon and stars, fish, birds, animals, and people.

If you don't have many children in your program, assign one child to each of these eight roles. If you have fewer than ten children altogether, cast Martha and God, and have the remaining children share the other eight roles.

Tell your actors that they'll play the role they've been assigned and need to think of an action that portrays their role. For instance, "light" could mime a giant flashlight, or your kids could place their hands on the sides of their heads and "beam" their brightest smiles.

Give actors 30 seconds to figure out how to play their roles, then play "A Good Thing" (track 1). Stop the CD after the segment ends.

SAY **Another wonderful performance! I felt like I was there in the beginning, when God created the heavens and the earth.**

Lead your kids in giving themselves a round of applause, then ask them to stay in their places. Ask kids to recall their roles and to tell a neighbor what they think it was like *before* God created the heavens and the earth—what it looked like, sounded like, tasted like, smelled like, felt like.

Give children a minute to talk, then tell kids you're going to turn off the lights so they can pretend it's before God created anything. When you turn on the lights, you'll ask them to resume acting out the parts of creation that they represented during the drama. When the lights come back on, tell children you'd like them to make appropriate noises for their part of creation too.

When you're sure everyone understands the directions, ask children to sit and get comfortable. Ask children to sit very still and to remain quiet for a few moments after you turn out the lights.

Turn off the lights, and let kids remain in the darkness for about 30 seconds.

SAY **"In the beginning God created the heavens and the earth."** Then, quickly, turn on the lights.

Encourage kids to act out what the world was like *after* God had created it.

Play a "before and after" game: When the lights are off, kids must be still and quiet. When you turn on the lights, they should act like noisy animals or growing

plants. Turn the lights on and off repeatedly, with just a few seconds of light and dark each time, to challenge the kids to quickly act out the "before" and "after" of creation.

After several rounds of lights-on, lights-off, use your attention-getting signal to return kids' attention to yourself. Ask BibleVenture Buddies to gather their children around them, and discuss the following questions:

Make life easy for your BibleVenture Buddies and yourself by making a copy of the questions for each leader. Then you won't have to keep interrupting the discussion flow to ask the next question.

● **What was it like to sit quietly in the dark? And then how did you feel after the lights came on?**

● **Why do you think God created all these different things?**

● **How do you feel about God when you think about him creating the heavens and the earth?**

● **Each time God created something new, he said it was good. How does that make you feel about God's creation?**

SAY **Before God got to work, there was nothing here. The beginning of the world happened when God began creating it. That's what our Venture Verse says.**

Lead kids in repeating the Venture Verse together: "In the beginning God created the heavens and the earth" (Genesis 1:1).

SAY **(BP) God's creation shows us his glory. Remember how wonderful and wise God is every time you think about what he created. Only God could create the universe from nothing, and make all of it good!**

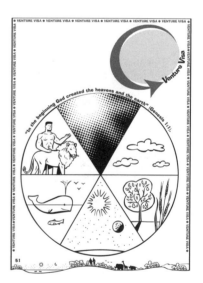

Have kids take out their Venture Visas and turn to the page that shows the circular progression of creation along with the Venture Verse. Ask BibleVenture Buddies to help distribute pens or pencils to the children.

SAY **Take a moment to think about one part of creation for which you're especially thankful. On your Venture Visa page, find the picture that's closest to the part of creation you have in mind.**

For example, if you're especially thankful for a friend or family member, find the picture that includes people. If you're especially thankful for flowers, find the picture that shows plants.

Ask BibleVenture Buddies to help any kids in their groups that need assistance.

SAY **Once you've found the picture that's closest to what you have in mind, circle it, then, in the upper left part of the page, write or draw what you're especially thankful for in that square.**

As kids write or draw, play soft instrumental music (track 16, "Instrumental Music for Prayer Time," is one option). As they work, move around the room and place a stamp or sticker on each child's page to signify that he or she has traveled to your Venture Center.

After a couple of minutes, turn off the music and get the children's attention again. Have kids put their Venture Visas aside, and ask BibleVenture Buddies to collect the pens and pencils and set them aside.

SAY **God created lots of good things, including me and you! I'm going to read about God's creation of people. Listen to what God says to the people.**

Open your Bible to Genesis 1:26-30, show kids the page, and then read aloud the Scripture passage.

ASK

● **What does creation tell us about God?** Call on a few volunteers and let them share their answers.

SAY **God gave us life, gave us good work to do, and gave us good foot to eat.**

ASK

● **What do you think it means that God made people in his image?** (For the word "image," substitute the word your Bible translation uses in Genesis 1:27.) Call on a few volunteers and let them share their answers.

SAY **When the Bible says we're made in the "image of God," that doesn't mean we look like God or have God's wisdom and power.**

Think about your shadow. If we only saw your shadow, we'd know a little bit about you. But your shadow is not the same as *you*.

In a way, people are like God's shadows. Because God created us in his image, others can know God a little bit by knowing us. But we are *not* God. Let's do an activity to help us think about what it means that we are created in God's image.

Have Venture Teams stand up and each choose one team member to be the leader. The other team members will play the "images" and stand facing the leader. Instruct the leaders to move slowly—pretending to eat or get dressed, for example. Their images should try to mirror the leaders' motions.

Play soft instrumental music (track 16, "Instrumental Music for Prayer Time," is one option) as kids mimic one another.

After 30 or 45 seconds, pause the music and have kids switch roles.

Play the music again as kids mimic one another. Have kids switch roles again so that everyone gets a chance to be a leader. Then have kids sit down to discuss the following questions in their Venture Teams.

If you have Venture Teams of more than six, consider saving time by having teams form trios for this mimic activity.

● **What was it like to be an image of the leader?**

● **How well did you mirror you leader's actions?**

SAY **You all did a great job as leaders and as images! You were a reflection of your leader, but you did not become your leader. That's what an image does: it reflects, but it doesn't replace what it's reflecting.**

Because God created us in his image, we are reflections of God. We are not and do not become God. Only God could create the heavens the earth. Only God could create you and me. That's why  **God's creation shows us his glory.**

The second chapter of Genesis tells us a little bit more about how God created people. We're going to put on another play with the CD to act out that scene.

Have kids volunteer to play "Adam," "God" (using the offstage flashlight again), "Eve," elephants, kangaroos, eagles, and frogs. You can cast as many elephants, kangaroos, eagles, and frogs as you need to ensure that everyone has a part to play. Encourage the animals to create motions to do when their animals are mentioned, and allow kids to dress up if they want to. Give "Eve" the flower lei, and give "Adam" a necktie.

Ask the child playing God to stand offstage again and shine a light onto the stage whenever "God" speaks on the CD. Ask Adam to stand off-center, toward the side of the stage from which the light portraying God will be coming. Ask Eve to stand offstage until she is "created," at which point she can join Adam onstage.

Have the other cast members stand in a row across the rest of the stage. Explain that Adam will be naming animals, falling asleep, and waking up to name animals again. Explain that the animals should wait until their animal is called and then make the motion they created for that creature.

 When kids understand their parts and are ready to go, play "Naming the Animals" (track 2). Stop the CD after the segment ends.

SAY **Wow! What great actors you are! Tell me what you would have named these creatures if you'd been there.**

Pause for volunteers to answer. Then explain that they are going to do the drama again so that kids can switch roles. Choose a different "Adam," "Eve," and "God." Be sure the props go to the kids playing those roles as well. Allow the kids playing animals to try new animal roles and create new animal motions.

When the kids are ready to go, play "Naming the Animals" (track 2). Stop the CD after the segment ends.

It's not essential that boys play male roles and girls play female roles. Remind kids that in a drama everything is pretend.

You can let children change costumes before they repeat the drama if you like. Just keep an eye on the time so that kids don't take so long preparing for the drama that they don't have time to *do* the drama!

Make life easy for your BibleVenture Buddies and yourself by making a copy of the questions for each leader. Then you won't have to keep interrupting the discussion flow to ask the next question.

SAY **Great job! It looked like Adam and Eve were having lots of fun with the special job God gave them to do.**

Ask BibleVenture Buddies to have their Venture Teams sit together to discuss the following questions.

ASK

● **Why do you think God gave people a job to do?**

● **Why do you think Adam wanted a friend?**

● **How did God show his love for creation in this play?**

● **What can creation help you remember about God?**

SAY **God is so powerful that he created the universe out of nothing, but he still cared about Adam. God didn't need Adam's help, but he knew people would feel better if they had a purpose—a job to do. And when Adam was lonely, God was so loving that he created just the right friend. (BP) God's creation shows us his glory. When we see what God has created, we can remember how much God loves us.**

It should be about time to move back to The Depot. Close your Venture Center with a short prayer, thanking God for his creation and for loving us so well. Then help BibleVenture Buddies escort the children back to The Depot for the closing.

If You Still Have Time...

If you finish before it's time to head back to The Depot, use this activity.

Read aloud Psalm 139:13-16 and discuss the fact that God created each and every person—including each child. To celebrate how fearfully and wonderfully we were made, lead children in an active rendition of "Head, Shoulders, Knees, and Toes" or "Dry Bones."

Drama Script

These are provided for your reference. They're on the CD; you don't need to reproduce them.

A Good Thing (track 1)

Announcer

The BibleVentures news channel interrupts our regularly scheduled program to bring you this breaking story. Martha, our reporter who is well-known for interviewing the rich and famous until they cry, has won an exclusive interview with a very special guest, the most highly respected artist of all time.

She's standing by now in front of a studio audience to bring you this special report, brought to you by the creative artists' group, Do-Art. Martha?

Martha

Thank you, friends, and welcome to our show. Today we have a special guest, the first and greatest artist of all time, who will tell us about his best work of art, the *entire universe*! Please give a round of applause to the Creator of the world, God himself! God, thank you so much for coming to our show.

God

Thank you, Martha. I'm pleased to be here.

Martha

Our audience is interested in hearing how you made the world. I've asked our Do-Art Drama Team of actors to act out the steps of creation as you describe them. Audience, please give a round of applause for our Do-Art Drama Team.

Now, God, why don't you tell us about the first day of creation?

God

In the beginning I created the heavens and the earth. Darkness was everywhere until I said, "Let there be light." I called the light "day," and the darkness, "night." And there was evening and morning, the first day. I saw that it was good.

Martha

Yes, it was a good thing. Our actors are waving their hands over their heads to illustrate the light. How lovely.

God

I said, "Let there be space between the waters to separate water from water." I called the space "sky." And there was evening and morning, the second day.

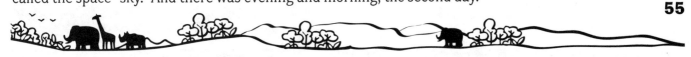

Martha

And that was a good thing too. Our actors are looking up into the sky. How exciting! Please tell us about the third day.

God

I said, "Let the land produce vegetation: plants and trees." And the land did produce plants and trees. And it was good.

Martha

Our actors are showing us plants bursting through the ground, and they're opening their hands like flowers opening up.

God

I said, "Let there be lights in the sky to separate the day from the night." I made two great lights. The sun and the moon. I also made the stars.

Martha

Actors, cover your eyes to shield them from all this light!

God

On the fifth day I said, "Let the water be filled with living creatures—like fish and whales and squids and shrimp—and let birds fly above the earth across the whole sky—eagles and sparrows and pelicans and hawks." And it was a good thing.

Martha

Some of the actors are swimming like fish, and some are flapping their arms like the wings of birds.

God

On the sixth day I said, "Let the land produce living creatures—livestock, like cows and pigs; creatures that move along the ground, like lizards and crocodiles; and wild animals of every kind, like lions and tigers and bears."

Martha

Oh, my! And now our actors are moving like animals. I think I see an elephant. Oh, is that a giraffe? And a bear. And even a kitten.

God

Also on the sixth day I decided to make—people! Maybe the actors can just move like themselves now. I said, "Let us make man in our image, in our likeness." I created man and woman.

Martha

Your creation—it's a very good thing. After all that work you must have been exhausted, just like our actors are exhausted!

God

Well, Martha, you know, I don't get tired. I am God, after all. But I wanted to spend some time just enjoying what I had created, so on the seventh day I rested from all my work. I blessed the seventh day and made it holy. Maybe the actors would like to sit down and rest now.

Martha

Audience, let's give God and our actors a round of applause for all they've shared with us today. Thank you, God, for this great world you created. It's a very good thing.

Naming the Animals (track 2)

God

So Adam, how do you like the Garden of Eden so far? Are you happy here?

Adam

Well, yeah, God, I am. I mean, you've given me all these trees and plants. And there are all these animals. But I'm a little lonely. I wish I had a friend of my own...

God

Speaking of animals, Adam, I have a job for you.

Adam

A job? What's a job?

God

Oh, that's right; you've never had a job before, have you? Well, a job is a special task. Your job is to name all the animals.

Adam

Cool! Sounds like fun.

God

Let's start with this creature here with the long nose.

Adam

Hmm, well, I could call it long-nosed, floppy-eared water-snorter.

God

That's a little long. Try something shorter.

Adam

I could call it—elephant!

God

Good, good, I like that name! Elephant it is! Let's look at this next animal with the pouch. Look how it jumps! What will you name it?

Adam

I could name it hoppy pocket.

God

Are you sure about that?

Adam

No, maybe not. I know! I'll call it kangaroo!

God

What about this animal? The one with the wings.

Adam

I might call it bald-headed sky flyer, but—I think I like eagle better.

God

Now here's a fun little creature. Look at its green skin and long tongue.

Adam

Forked-tongue fly zapper. No, ribitting lily pad dweller. No. Oh, oh, I know—frog!

God

Frog, a lovely name.

Adam

God, I like all these animals, but I still don't have a friend. I'd like someone to help me name these animals. I'd like someone who can talk to me and enjoy this wonderful garden with me. I don't mean to complain, God. You've given me so much. But it just seems like something is missing...

God

Adam, it's not good for you to be alone. Lie down and go to sleep. Yes, go to sleep.

Now, while you're sleeping, I'm going to make you a helper suitable for you. I'll just take one of your ribs here, and do a little work here, and, yes, I think she's ready. OK, Adam, wake up!

Eve

Hi. Who are you?

Adam

I'm Adam. Who are you?

Eve

I don't know!

God

Maybe you should give her a name too.

Adam

I will call you Eve. Thanks, God, for giving me a friend!

God

You're welcome. Now why don't you two go name some more animals?

Adam and Eve

'Bye, God! See you later!

Eve

Did you see that animal with long ears and a fuzzy tail? What should we call *that* one?

Venture Center Two:

God's creation shows us his glory.

Venture Verse: "In the beginning God created the heavens and the earth" (Genesis 1:1).

Welcome!

You'll be leading the Art Venture Center for the next four weeks. One great piece of news is that preparing for the four weeks is easy because you prepare just *one* week's lesson—and present it four times!

Here's how your Venture Center works: Each week children gather at The Depot for a time of opening and adventure. While at The Depot, children will get together in their Venture Teams, and then one group (it could be one Venture Team or several, but each will have an adult leader) will travel to your Venture Center. This group of children will stay with you for 40 minutes, then return to The Depot for a time of closing and celebration.

In the weeks that follow, different groups of children will come to your Venture Center. You'll repeat the same activity for all four weeks, each week with a different group of children. This allows you to prepare just once and have four weeks of meaningful interaction with children as you lead them closer to God!

Your Venture Center

During this BibleVenture, children will learn about God's creation. Children will discover that God's creation shows us his glory.

You'll notice that the Bible Point, "God's creation shows us his glory," is mentioned several times in your lesson. That's by intent, and it's important that you reinforce the point by saying it each time—or even more often. By the end of this BibleVenture, children will have considered what it means that God's creation reveals his glory—his wisdom, power, and love.

In your Venture Center, children will use their creative skills to craft a mobile of the earth, sun, and moon while they learn about God's glory as the Creator. The art projects will help children tell others that God created the heavens and earth.

Your enthusiasm for this Venture Center and the art project will be passed on to the children you meet each week. Greet them with excitement, encourage them to join in, and have fun!

Preparation

Before children arrive, gather these supplies:

- Bible
- CD player
- *BibleVentures: Creation* CD
- a stamp or small stickers to mark in visas (glow-in-the-dark stars, if you can find them)
- paint shirts
- foam balls that are about 5 inches in diameter
- paintbrushes
- yarn cut into 1-foot pieces
- foam or plastic bowls or muffin cups for paint
- blue and green tempera paint
- paper or plastic cups for water
- water
- plain white paper towels cut into strips 1- to 2-inches wide
- glue solution (one cup of nontoxic glue mixed with three cups of water)
- balloons that, when blown up, are small and round
- wax paper
- white paper plates
- yellow, orange, and red crayons or markers
- staplers or rolls of tape
- crepe paper streamers cut into strips that are 3 or 4 inches long
- hole punches
- hangers
- plastic grocery sacks
- newspaper or newsprint
- tape
- rags or sponges to wipe up spills
- washcloths or wet wipes to clean hands
- scissors
- pens or pencils

Before children arrive, make one finished mobile of the earth, sun, and moon. You'll also need to prepare a work area in your room. Place newsprint or

Establish a nonverbal signal to use to direct kids' attention back to yourself. Suggestion: Clap your hands, flick the lights, blow on a wooden train whistle, or use another unusual sound maker that won't be mistaken in the midst of discussion. Practice the signal several times until kids recognize it and respond to it.

newspaper over the surface, and tape it down so kids won't slip on it and so it won't slide apart to reveal the surface.

Also gather paint shirts—old T-shirts or button-down shirts that kids can put on over their clothes. You may also want to provide additional yarn or ribbon to tie back long or full sleeves or long hair so that they don't fall into paint or glue.

Before kids arrive, cut the paper towels, yarn, and streamers. Mix the glue solution and place it in several bowls. Also fill several bowls with the green and blue paint. Fill plastic or paper cups with water for kids to clean their paintbrushes.

Place the art project supplies where children will have easy access to them.

The Venture Center

Welcome children as they enter your Venture Center. Explain that kids will explore the story of creation through an art project.

SAY **We're learning how God created the heavens and the earth, and we're also discovering that**  **God's creation shows us his glory.**

Before God created the universe, there was nothing here. Nothing at all! But God made land and seas, the sun and moon, and plants and animals and people. God filled the emptiness with our beautiful world! The book of Genesis, the very first book in the Bible, tells us about it.

Read aloud Genesis 1:1-2. Ask the children to cover their ears and close their eyes as they try to imagine what the nothingness was like. Ask them to open their eyes and uncover their ears when they think 45 seconds have passed.

Children will vary widely as to when they open their eyes (their strategy will be to count to 45). When all eyes are open (you may have to nudge a few children who are counting very slowly!), read aloud Genesis 1:3-5. Play "Light Song" (track 3) on the CD in the background as you read.

ASK

● **After being in darkness for so long, what do you think it was like to be in the light?**

Read aloud Genesis 1:6-13. Play "Water Waves" (track 4) on the CD as you read.

SAY **With the growth of plants and the separation of the sea and the land, God created our blue and green planet Earth. God is so powerful that he made this very planet on which we live. He made it just right for us!**

Hold up the earth you created out of the foam ball.

SAY **We're going to start our art project by making the earth. When you look at it, you can remember that BP God's creation shows us his glory. You can even use your earth to tell other people that God created the heavens and the earth.**

Ask BibleVenture Buddies to collect the following supplies for his or her Venture Team:

● 1 foam ball per child

● 1 paintbrush per child

● 1 piece of yarn per child

● a bowl or cup of water for the group to share

● a bowl of green paint and a bowl of blue paint for the group to share

Be sure children are seated at the area you've protected from spills, and ask BibleVenture Buddies to help put paint shirts on the kids and tie back long sleeves and hair.

Have children make globes by painting green paint for land and blue paint for the oceans. Encourage them to use paint sparingly so that the globes will dry and the foam won't deteriorate with too much wet paint.

As children work, play the *BibleVentures: Creation* CD.

Circulate to offer assistance as needed. As children finish painting, help them tie the yarn around their globes. You'll want to tie the yarn so that most of the length will be left to attach the globe to a hanger to create a mobile.

Have kids write their names on the newspaper that's covering the work surface and set their globes next to their names. If children need to wash up, ask BibleVenture Buddies to help them.

After about ten minutes, stop the CD and get children's attention. Ask them to put aside anything they're working on for now.

ASK

● **Why do you think we need this planet Earth to live?**

Call on a few volunteers, and affirm their suggestions.

SAY **Your globes are looking good enough to live on! After God made the earth so that plants, animals, and people could live here, he got back to work. Let's see what the Bible says God did next.**

Read aloud Genesis 1:14-19.

ASK

● **Why do we need the sun?**

● **Why do we need the moon and stars?**

Affirm the suggestions offered by students, then ask Venture Teams to circle up with their BibleVenture Buddies and to discuss:

● **When you look at the sun, moon, and stars, what do you think about God?**

Give Venture Teams about 90 seconds to talk.

SAY **The sun is a super-hot, flaming ball. If the earth were just a little bit closer to the sun, it would be too hot. Plants, people, and animals wouldn't be able to live here. If the earth were just a little bit farther from the sun, it would be too cold for plants, people, and animals.**

Have children take out their Venture Visas and turn to the page that shows a picture of the sun, moon, and stars. Ask BibleVenture Buddies to help distribute pens or pencils to the children.

SAY **God made sure that the earth was just the right distance from the sun. So when we look at the sun, moon, and stars, we can think of how wise and powerful God is.** **BP** **God's creation shows us his glory.**

In the space on the picture, write two or three words that you think about God when you see what he created. For example, if creation helps you

If some kids finish earlier than others, allow them to be helpers. For example, they can clean up the paint and paintbrushes as other children are finishing up or can help wipe up any spills. Or if you'd rather, early finishers can simply move away from the work area and sing songs with the CD.

65

to remember that God is strong, you could write "strong" or draw a muscular arm on the picture.

Allow children time to do this. As they work, move around the room and place a stamp or sticker on each child's page to signify that they've traveled to your Venture Center. Afterward, have kids set aside their Venture Visas.

Hold up the moon and sun you created.

SAY **Let's make a moon and sun to go with our planet Earth. Then we can always remember how God put the sun, moon, and Earth in just the right places.**

We'll work on the moon first, and then we'll make the sun.

Have BibleVenture Buddies return the blue and green paint, the paintbrushes, and the cups of water. Have them pick up the following items to take back to their Venture Teams:

- strips of paper towels
- a bowl of white glue solution for the group to share
- 1 balloon per child
- 1 piece of yarn per child
- 1 sheet of wax paper per child

Before kids start, ask BibleVenture Buddies to make sure that the work space is ready and that kids' sleeves or long hair is still tied back securely.

Ask BibleVenture Buddies to help their kids blow up and tie off their balloons. Show kids how to dip a paper towel strip into the glue solution, pulling the strip between the index and middle finger to remove unnecessary liquid, and then wrap the strip around the balloon.

Tell kids to be sure *not* to cover the tied end of the balloon since they'll need to tie a piece of yarn there. Otherwise, kids can add paper towel strips until their balloon is covered.

Though this sounds easy, kids may have trouble with slipping paper towel strips and excess liquid. Circulate to offer assistance. If their moons get too wet, kids can add dry paper towel strips. Ask BibleVenture Buddies to help children and to help clean up spills as they occur.

As children work, play the *BibleVentures: Creation* CD. As kids finish, have them tie one end of the piece of yarn around the tied end of their balloons and then set the moon on the square of wax paper to begin drying.

After no more than ten minutes, have kids set aside what they're working on and wash their hands. Ask BibleVenture Buddies to clear away the papier-mâché supplies and gather the materials their groups need to make the sun. They'll need the following supplies:

- 1 paper plate per child
- crayons or markers for the group to share
- 1 stapler or roll of tape
- strips of streamers
- 1 hole punch
- 1 hanger per child
- 1 length of yarn per child
- 1 plastic grocery sack per child

Have kids color their paper plates, front and back, to create a sun. Then allow each child to attach a few streamers to the edge of the plate as the sun's rays. If you're using a stapler for this, only allow BibleVenture Buddies to staple streamer strips for kids.

Also ask BibleVenture Buddies to punch a hole in an edge of the plate and help kids tie one end of a piece of yarn through the hole.

As kids finish their suns, help them to assemble their mobiles by tying their sun, moon, and earth to a hanger. As kids work, ask them to discuss the following questions with their BibleVenture Buddies.

ASK

- **What was it like to create this sun, moon, and earth?**

- **How do you think God felt about the new things he created?**

- **Was this art project difficult to do? What does that make you think about what God accomplished?**

When five minutes of your Venture Center remains, have kids stop what they're doing, write their names on their projects, take off the paint shirts, remove any yarn that's tying back hair and long sleeves, and wash their hands.

SAY **God's creation shows us his glory. Only God is wise and powerful enough to create the heavens and the earth. God did it just right, with no mistakes.**

You can hang your mobile in your room to remember how amazing God is, or you can give your mobile to a friend and tell the story of God's amazing creation.

Because the papier-mâché will take a day or two to dry, have kids wrap their "moons" in the wax paper. Kids can put their mobiles in a plastic bag to carry them home.

It should be about time to move back to The Depot. Close with prayer, thanking God for creating the earth, the sun, and the moon just the right way. Then escort the children back to The Depot for the closing.

If You Still Have Time...

If you finish before it's time to head back to The Depot, use the following activity.

Have children use their completed projects to talk about God's creation. Ask volunteers to reread the account from Genesis 1:1-19 and then tell why each part of the creation is important to our lives. Then have children form pairs and practice telling each other what creation shows them about God. Encourage kids to use their mobiles to share what they learned with friends and family.

Venture Center Three:  The Games Center

God's creation shows us his glory. BP

Venture Verse: "In the beginning God created the heavens and the earth" (Genesis 1:1).

Welcome!

You'll be leading the Games Venture Center for the next four weeks. One great piece of news is that preparing for the four weeks is easy because you prepare just *one* week's lesson—and present it four times!

Here's how your Venture Center works: Each week children gather at The Depot for a time of opening and adventure. While at The Depot, children will get together in their Venture Teams, and then one group (it could be one Venture Team or several, but each will have an adult leader) will travel to your Venture Center. This group of children will stay with you for 40 minutes, then return to The Depot for a time of closing and celebration.

In the weeks that follow, different groups of children will come to your Venture Center. You'll repeat the same activity for all four weeks, each week with a different group of children. This allows you to prepare just once and have four weeks of meaningful interaction with children as you lead them closer to God!

Your Venture Center

During this BibleVenture, children will learn about God's creation. Children will discover that God's creation shows us God's glory.

You'll notice that the Bible Point, "God's creation shows us his glory," is mentioned several times in your lesson. That's by intent, and it's important that you reinforce the point by saying it each time—or even more often. By the end of this BibleVenture, children will have considered what it means that God's creation reveals his glory—his wisdom, power, and love.

In your Venture Center, children will use games to explore the fact that God gave purpose to his creation. When you use these activities, game time becomes learning time, too!

Children *love* to play games, but too often game time is also when kids discover that they're not fast enough, not tall enough, and not as coordinated as everyone else. And anyone who has been picked last for a softball game knows how humiliation feels.

That's why your role leading this Venture Center is so important. You'll make sure that game time is positive, that everybody plays, that everybody cooperates, and that nobody goes home feeling like a loser. The goal is for kids to play *with* one another, not *against* one another. It's a new concept for some people. Your enthusiasm for this Venture Center and the games will be passed on to the children you meet each week. Greet them with excitement, encourage them to join in, and have fun!

Preparation

Before children arrive, gather these supplies:
- Bible
- a stamp or small stickers to mark in visas
- flashlight with a bright beam
- an assortment of stuffed animals and/or pictures of animals
- pens or pencils

The Venture Center

Warmly welcome children to the Venture Center.

SAY **We're going on a wonderful adventure today to learn about the beginning of the world! Our Venture Verse, Genesis 1:1, tells us something very important about that beginning. It says, "In the beginning God created the heavens and the earth."** Ask kids to repeat the Venture Verse with you.

For our adventure, we're going to play some fun games that'll help us think about God's creation. We'll learn that  **God's creation shows us his glory.**

God is so powerful that when he wanted to create light, he only had to say, "Let there be light." After God made night and day, he separated the sky from the ocean. Next God gathered the water together so that dry ground appeared on the earth. God called the dry ground "land."

ASK

- **What different types of land can you think of?**

Have kids call out different types of land—mountains, plains, deserts, swamps, jungles, and valleys, for example.

SAY **Let's play our first game to celebrate all the different kinds of land God made.**

Creation Crash!

Have kids stand in a large circle. Choose four or five different types of land, and have kids "count off" by assigning them one of the types of land. One child will be "mountain," the next will be "swamp," the next will be "desert," the next will be "jungle," then the next will be "mountain," then "swamp," and so on until every child in the circle has been assigned a land type.

Stand in the center of the circle. Explain that when you call out a particular type of land—mountains, for example—everyone assigned that type will move out of their space in the circle, cross the circle, and try to find a new space. The catch is that *you* also will try to find a space, so one person will be left without a space. That person must stand in the middle of the circle and call out a land type. A person also may call out the word "creation!" When this happens, everyone must run across the circle and find a new spot.

When kids understand how to play, start the game. Help children remember to call out the different types of land that were assigned. After a few minutes of play, have everyone sit down. Ask BibleVenture Buddies to gather their Venture Teams together for a discussion.

ASK

● **Why do you think God made all those different kinds of land?**

● **What plants and animals live in the mountains? the desert? the swamp? the jungle?**

SAY **When God made the world, he made it just right. Everything he made had a special reason for being. Listen to what the Bible says about the special reasons God made the land.**

Read aloud Genesis 1:11-13, 29-30.

ASK

● **What was the special reason God made the land?**

● **What things does the land provide for us?**

SAY **Different plants grow in different types of soil and weather. Some plants need lots of sun and dry weather; they do well in deserts but would die in jungles. Other plants need lots of rain; they would die in deserts.**

This game is a fun one to play with a large group. If you have more than 20 or 25 kids, however, you may want to have them form more than one circle for this game.

Make life easy for your BibleVenture Buddies and yourself by making a copy of the questions for each leader. Then you won't have to keep interrupting the discussion flow to ask the next question.

ASK

● **How do you feel about God, knowing that he made different types of land so that lots of different types of plants could grow?**

SAY  **God's creation shows us his glory. God is so wise and good to create all these different types of land so that different types and plants could live on earth.**

God didn't stop creating after he made the land and the plants, though. Let's find out what God did next. Listen carefully to see if you can hear the special reason God made these next things.

Read aloud Genesis 1:14-19, then ask Venture Teams to discuss the following:

● **What are the special jobs of the sun, the moon, and the stars?**

● **What would your life be like if there were no sun and no moon?**

SAY **In our next game, we'll see the difference between the light of the sun and the moon.**

Chase the Moonbeam

Have kids stand up and form one large line. They should stand so they can put their hands on the waist of the person in front of them, like a bunny-hop line or a train.

Explain that they are going to walk around the room and try to stay connected with one another. You're going to turn off the lights, and the leader must follow the "moon"—a beam of light from a flashlight that you'll shine on the floor. When the "sun comes up"—when you turn on the overhead lights—the leader must go to the back of the line.

When kids understand how to play, have them begin walking around the room, snaking back and forth. Then turn off the overhead lights, and point the beam of light from a bright flashlight on the floor so that you lead the line of children around the room. Turn on the overhead lights again so a different child can lead.

Play for several minutes, giving as many kids as possible a chance to lead. Then ask BibleVenture Buddies to help their Venture Team members form trios for the following discussion.

ASK

● **What was it like to walk in the moonlight? in the sunlight?**

● **How do you feel about the sun, moon, and stars now that you understand one reason why God created them?**

If you have enough space, have kids form groups of six or seven for this game. If you play this way, you'll need a BibleVenture Buddy to lead each line with a flashlight. Remind the BibleVenture Buddies not to cause collisions with other groups.

● How do you feel about the God who was wise and powerful enough to create the sun, moon, and stars?

SAY **BP** **God's creation shows us his glory. God was so wise and powerful that he knew the earth would need the sun, moon, and stars.**

God also knew the earth would need lots of animals! So in the beginning, he created them, too. As I read from Genesis, listen for the different types of animals you hear about.

Read aloud Genesis 1:20-25. Ask kids to report what different types of animals were mentioned.

SAY **God sure thought of a lot of different animals—animals that fly, swim, stand on feet, slither along the ground, and so on. Let's see if we can come up with some new animals.**

Creature Features

Explain that each trio will link their bodies together somehow to make a brand new animal. For example, one child could stand arms akimbo, one child could sit on her knees and hook her head through the standing child's right arm, and the last child could lie on the floor and place his feet through the standing child's left arm. Tell trios that they must create the new animal, give it a name, and be prepared to tell the group what its special job is.

Give children several minutes to create their new animals. After several minutes, have each trio present its animal, the animal's name, and the animal's special job to the large group.

Have kids sit with their trios again to discuss the following questions.

ASK

● **Why do you think God created animals?**

● **How hard or easy was it to think of new animals?**

● **How hard or easy was it to think of a special job for your animal?**

● **What do you think it was like for God to create all those different kinds of animals?**

SAY **You'd think God would've run out of ideas by the time he was done creating all those animals. But God is amazing, and he wasn't finished yet! Let's read about one more thing God created. Listen again for the special job.**

Venture view

If you have more than 15 or 18 children, save time by having trios share their animals in more than one group.

73

Read aloud Genesis 1:26-28. Then explain that the second chapter in Genesis gives a little more detail about the creation of people. Remind children to continue listening for the special job, then read aloud Genesis 2:7-8, 15.

ASK

● **What special jobs did God give to people?**

● **Why do you think God wanted people to do these jobs?**

SAY **Let's play a fun game of charades to think about all the different kinds of jobs people do.**

Name That Job

Have kids form groups of five or six. Each group should find some space in the room apart from the other groups. Explain that each child will have the opportunity to think of a job and act it out for his or her group members, who will then try to guess what the job is.

When kids understand how to play, start the game. Make sure every child has a chance to act out a job; if you have time, allow them to play again.

Then have children sit down with their Venture Teams to discuss these questions.

ASK

● **Have you ever been given a special job to do? What?**

● **How did it feel to be trusted to do a special job?**

● **How does it make you feel to know that God created you for a special job?**

SAY **When God created people, he told them to "rule over the fish of the sea and the birds of the air and over every living creature that moves on the ground"** (Genesis 1:28). **That means we are supposed to take care of those creatures. In our last game, we'll see how well we can take care of some animals.**

Missing Mammals

Have kids gather with their Venture Teams. Give each group a pile of about six or seven stuffed animals and/or pictures of animals.

Explain that children should try to remember every animal in the pile. Children will close their eyes, and the BibleVenture Buddies will then remove one of the animals. When children open their eyes, they should try to identify which animal is missing. To guess which animal is missing, kids must make that animal's sound—a "moo" or a "meow," for example.

When everyone understands how to play, ask children to close their eyes and BibleVenture Buddies to remove one of the animals. Allow BibleVenture Buddies to repeat the game with their groups for several minutes.

When you have about ten minutes left to your Venture Center, or when kids have played the game a few times, get everyone's attention again. Have children discuss these questions in the Venture Teams.

ASK

● **What was it like to keep track of these animals?**

● **Have you ever had to take care of a pet or even baby-sit a child? If so, what was it like to be responsible for it?**

● **Since God told us to rule over the animals, does that mean we can treat God's creation any way we want? Explain.**

SAY **God created the heavens and the earth. The Bible says everything in the world actually belongs to God** (Psalm 24:1). **God trusts us to look after what he created.**

ASK

● **How does it feel to know that God trusts you and me to care for his creation?**

● **What are some ways you can care for God's creation next week?**

Ask children to take out their Venture Visas. Ask BibleVenture Buddies to help distribute pens or pencils to the children.

SAY **Turn to the page where you see the people carrying the earth. On the earth, write or draw one way you'll care for God's creation this week. For example, you might write, "I'll pick up trash I see on the sidewalk" or "I'll plant a flower."**

As children work in their groups, move around the room and place a stamp or sticker on each child's page to signify that they've traveled to your Venture Center.

SAY **Remember,**  **God's creation shows us his glory. When we care for creation, we are making sure that creation will be around forever to remind us of God's wisdom, power, and love.**

Close with prayer, thanking God for trusting each of us with the special responsibility of caring for his creation. Ask God to help the children follow through on their ideas to care for creation.

Make life easy for your BibleVenture Buddies and yourself by making a copy of the questions for each leader. Then you won't have to keep interrupting the discussion flow to ask the next question.

When children finish this, it should be about time to move back to The Depot. Escort the children back to The Depot for the closing.

If You Still Have Time...

If you finish before it's time to head back to The Depot, use the following activity.

Have children close their eyes while you hide several of the animals from the previous game around the room. Distribute a flashlight to each Venture Team. Turn off the lights, and challenge kids to use only the light of the "moon" to find the lost animals. When kids have found the animals or are stumped, turn on the lights. Then play again!

Venture Center Four:

God's creation shows us his glory. BP

Venture Verse: "In the beginning God created the heavens and the earth" (Genesis 1:1).

Welcome!

You'll be leading the Audio-Visual Venture Center for the next four weeks. One great piece of news is that preparing for the four weeks is easy because you prepare just *one* week's lesson—and present it four times!

Here's how your Venture Center works: Each week children gather at The Depot for a time of opening and adventure. While at The Depot, children will get together in their Venture Teams, and then one group (it could be one Venture Team or several, but each will have an adult leader) will travel to your Venture Center. This group of children will stay with you for 40 minutes, then return to The Depot for a time of closing and celebration.

In the weeks that follow, different groups of children will come to your Venture Center. You'll repeat the same activity for all four weeks, each week with a different group of children. This allows you to prepare just once and have four weeks of meaningful interaction with children as you lead them closer to God!

Your Venture Center

During this BibleVenture, children will learn about God's creation. Children will discover that God's creation shows us his glory.

You'll notice that the Bible Point, "God's creation shows us his glory," is mentioned several times in your lesson. That's by intent, and it's important that you reinforce the point by saying it each time—or even more often. By the end of this BibleVenture, children will have considered what it means that God's creation reveals his glory—his wisdom, power, and love.

In your Venture Center, children will explore the living things God created through your use of audio-visual equipment. Even young children today spend lots of time in front of a TV or listening to music, so they respond well to electronically generated images and sounds. Children in your Venture Center will

Before your Venture Center, set up the equipment you'll be using and run through the activities once to ensure that you won't be fumbling with electronics as children wait impatiently.

see and hear the staggering variety of God's creation, which reflects God's wisdom and power.

Your enthusiasm for this Venture Center and the activities will be passed on to the children you meet each week. Greet them with excitement, encourage them to join in, and have fun!

Preparation

Before children arrive, gather these supplies:

- CD player
- *BibleVentures: Creation* CD
- a stamp or small stickers to mark in visas
- Bible
- pens and pencils
- crayons
- baggies
- small notebooks or index cards
- small magnifying glasses, if possible (Party or craft stores often carry inexpensive, small magnifying glasses as party favors.)
- paper towel tubes
- remote control
- animal stickers
- laptop computer with PowerPoint presentation software and the ability to project the PowerPoint images on a screen

Establish a nonverbal signal to use to direct kids' attention back to yourself. Suggestion: Clap your hands or flick the lights, or blow on a wooden train whistle or other unusual sound maker that won't be mistaken in the midst of discussion. Practice the signal several times until kids recognize it and respond to it.

Put together small bags of supplies for the kids to carry "on safari" with them. Include small notebooks or index cards, pens or pencils, crayons, little magnifying glasses, and paper towel tubes as "telescopes."

You'll also need to hide one animal sticker per child around the room. Be sure that some hiding places aren't too difficult for the younger children to find.

The Venture Center

Warmly welcome children to your Venture Center.

SAY **We have an exciting adventure ahead as we explore God's creation. In this Venture Center, you actually become scientists on safari. What is a safari?** Pause for kids to share their ideas. If necessary, explain that a safari is an expedition—in this case an expedition to discover information about God's creation.

Our adventure is going to take us to see the tiniest parts of God's creation and some really big parts of God's creation. Through our exploration, we'll

see that **God's creation shows us his glory. Only God, with his power and wisdom and love, could create such a magnificent world. Let's get this safari started! First, every good scientist needs a few tools.**

Distribute the baggies of supplies to kids. You may want to point out the paper tubes, calling them "telescopes."

SAY **Our Venture Verse, Genesis 1:1, says, "In the beginning God created the heavens and the earth."**

God is so powerful that he created an entire universe full of planets and stars—huge things! But God is also so wise that he built this universe from tiny, tiny "bricks" that we can't even see. To explore some of those tiny things, we're going to have to get a lot smaller. I brought my Acme Shrinks-a-lot. Hold up the remote control, and point it at the children. **Are you ready to shrink? Here we go!**

Play "Wavy Ray" (track 5) on the CD, and walk around the room to "zap" all the kids with the remote control. Encourage kids to pretend to wither and shrink. Don't forget to zap yourself! Then turn off the CD.

Turn off the lights, and project the first image from the "Wonders of Creation" PowerPoint presentation (track 17 on the *BibleVentures: Creation* CD) onto the wall.

SAY **We must have shrunk to a very, very, very tiny size if we're able to see an atom. God made every element in the world from these teeny-tiny atoms, but they're much, much, much tinier even than a grain of sand.**

Project the second image.

SAY **This is a cell. A cell is the smallest part of any living thing, so God created your body with millions of tiny cells like this one! Again, cells are much, much tinier than a grain of sand.**

Turn on the lights.

SAY **Isn't God amazing? It's hard to believe that God built the world with such tiny things. We can learn so much about creation by looking at the small things. And the more we learn about creation, the more we learn about God.**

Use your magnifying glasses to find and look at something tiny—maybe a hair on your arm or a piece of dirt you find on the ground. When you find something tiny, draw a picture of it in your notebook.

Give kids a minute to do this.

For an extra "wow" experience, borrow a microscope and allow kids to look close up at a hair, a thin slice of potato, or a leaf.

ASK

● **Why do you think God made such tiny things?**

● **What other tiny parts of God's creation are important?**

Listen to kids' suggestions, and affirm answers.

SAY **God created the big things—the sun, moon, stars, land, and seas—but he created them by using small things. Small things such as cells and atoms—and even children—are very, very important!** (BP) **God's creation shows us his glory. Because of the way God made the world, we know God doesn't overlook the small things.**

Let's grow a bit more so we can actually look firsthand at some of God's creation. I'll set my Acme Shrinks-a-lot to "reverse."

Play "Wavy Ray" (track 5) on the CD, and walk around the room to "zap" all the kids with the remote control. Encourage kids to pretend to grow a bit. Don't forget to zap yourself!

Turn off the lights, then play the "Floral Fields" (track 6) segment of the CD. Show the next four slides while you read aloud Genesis 1:11-12. Encourage children to look closely at the plants, and after you read the passage, to call out the differences between the plants that they see.

Then tell kids that they're going to find a *real* plant to study. Turn off the CD player, and turn on the lights. Ask BibleVenture Buddies to take their groups outside for just two minutes and help each child find a leaf, a blade of grass, a flower, or another plant. For fun, encourage kids to use their magnifying glasses or telescopes as they search.

After two minutes, call the kids back inside. Show kids how to make a rubbing by placing the plant on a hard surface such as a table, then placing a piece of paper from their notebooks over the plant and rubbing the paper with the side of a crayon.

After a minute, have kids place their notebooks, crayons, and plants in their baggies.

SAY **While we're this size, we should look for other small things—like bugs!**

Turn off the lights, and play the "Bugs Galore" (track 7) segment of the CD. Show the next three images of insects, and ask children to name all the different colors and shapes they see.

SAY **Remember, there wasn't even color before God created it. Look at these wild colors and shapes.**

We probably don't want to stay bug size for too long. We don't want to get squished! I'll use the Acme Shrinks-a-lot on "reverse" to make us a bit bigger.

 Play "Wavy Ray" (track 5) on the CD, and walk around the room to "zap" all the kids with the remote control. Encourage kids to pretend to grow a bit. Don't forget to zap yourself!

 Play the "Chirps and Chatters" (track 8) segment of the CD.

ASK

● **Can you tell by the sounds what size we are now? You're now about the size of a bird!**

Ask kids to circle up with their Venture Buddies and discuss:

● **Imagine if God had made a world without any sounds. What would that be like?**

● **Imagine if God had made a world with just one sound so that everyone beeped the same note all the time. What would that be like?**

Turn off the CD.

SAY **Now listen to another sound: the sound of my voice as I read about God's creation.**

Read aloud Genesis 1:20-22, and show the next five slides. Then show the slides again, but challenge kids to make up sounds for each of the birds shown.

ASK

● **What was it like to make up new sounds for these birds?**

● **What will you remember about God when you hear the birds singing?**

SAY **God created so many different sounds when he created the heavens and the earth.** **(BP)** **God's creation shows us his glory.**

 Play the "Froggy Sounds" (track 9) segment of the CD.

SAY **Whoa—I hear some totally different sounds now!**

Show the next four slides, and ask children to call out the colors of the frogs and the colors of the leaves in each slide.

SAY **God even thought of ways to help some pretty helpless creatures hide. Little green frogs are hard to see on green leaves, and little brown frogs are hard to see on brown leaves.**

Turn off the CD, and turn on the lights. Have children pretend to be frogs by trying to find something that's a similar color to their clothing, hopping to it,

If it's not practical for kids to go outside for plants—due to bad weather, for example—bring real or fake leaves and flowers to the Venture Center. Before children arrive, sprinkle them around the room so kids can find them.

and standing next to it. For example, a child with a white shirt could stand in front of a white wall to "disappear."

After a minute, call the kids back.

SAY **Frogs may not be smart, but God gave them a good way to disappear! You all did a great job of disappearing, but I think it's time for us to get back to our normal size.**

Play "Wavy Ray" (track 5) on the CD, and walk around the room to "zap" all the kids with the remote control. Encourage kids to pretend to grow a bit. Don't forget to zap yourself!

Turn off the lights. Read aloud Genesis 1:24-25, and show the next five slides. Ask children to name their favorite animals.

SAY **God's creation shows us his glory. God is so wise, powerful, and loving that he provided for us through some of the animals. Some, like horses and cows, help us with our work. Others, like birds, carry seeds from place to place so that plants grow all over the world. Bees carry pollen and help make flowers. Everything God made is an important part of creation.**

After God created the light, sky, sea, land, plants, sun, moon, stars, fish, birds, and all other animals, God created people. God called the man Adam, and he gave Adam the job of naming the animals.

Show kids the mammal slides again, and have them shout out their own ideas about what the animals should have been called.

SAY **It's almost the end of our scientific safari. But no safari is complete without a picture of an animal. Use your "telescopes" to find in this room an animal sticker to put in your safari notebook.**

Give kids a minute to find the stickers you placed around the room. Then ask them to sit with their Venture Teams for the following discussion.

ASK

● **On our safari, you saw a lot of different things God created. What do you find most amazing about God's creation?**

● **What does God's creation tell you about him?**

● **What are some amazing things about God?**

● **What does it mean to you that you can talk to the God who created the heavens and the earth?**

Make life easy for your BibleVenture Buddies and yourself by making a copy of the questions for each leader. Then you won't have to keep interrupting the discussion flow to ask the next question.

Have children take out their Venture Visas and open to the page that shows a child sitting at the trunk of a tree.

SAY **In the blank space inside the tree, write a prayer to God. You can say anything to God.**

As children work, move around the room and place a stamp or a sticker on each child's page to signify that they've traveled to your Venture Center.

Have children take out their Venture Visas and open to the page that shows a tree.

As children work, move around the room and place a stamp or a sticker on each child's page to signify that they've traveled to your Venture Center.

When children finish this, it should be about time to move back to The Depot. Close your Venture Center with a short prayer, thanking God for showing us his glory through creation. Then escort the children back to The Depot for the closing.

If You Still Have Time...

If you finish before it's time to head back to The Depot, use the following activity.

If you have the time, know-how, and supplies, take digital photos of the Venture Teams and immediately download them to the computer. Read aloud Genesis 1:26-27 while you show the pictures to the children.

Otherwise, let children choose slides they want to see again. Encourage kids to give all the animals new names and sounds.

His Blessings Go Rolling Along

God is great; God is good.

I will praise him like I should,

For his blessings go rolling along.

Every day, every night,

I will praise him for his might,

For his blessings go rolling along.

For his love, for his grace,

I will shower him with praise,

For his blessings go rolling along.

Let us sing, let us shout,

Or the rocks will all cry out,

For his blessings go rolling along.

(Chorus)

For he sets me free,

Sent his Son to die for me.

Count all his blessings loud and strong!

(2! 3! 4! 5!)

So where'r I go, I'll let the whole world know

That his blessings go rolling along.

Doxology

Praise God,

From whom all blessings flow;

Praise him,

All creatures here below;

Praise him above, ye heavenly host;

Praise Father, Son, and Holy Ghost.

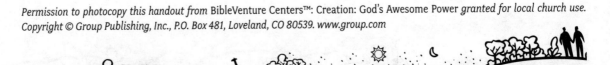

Song Lyrics

Hymn of Praise

Praise the Lord! Ye heavens, adore him.

Praise him, angels in the height.

Sun and moon, rejoice before him.

Praise him, all ye stars of light.

Praise the Lord! For he hath spoken.

Worlds his mighty voice obeyed.

Laws which never shall be broken,

For their guidance he hath made.

I Sing the Mighty Power of God

I sing the mighty pow'r of God

That made the mountains rise,

That spread the flowing seas abroad

And built the lofty skies.

I sing the wisdom that ordained

The sun to rule the day.

The moon shines full at God's command,

And all the stars obey.

I sing the goodness of the Lord

That filled the earth with food.

God formed the creatures with a word,

And then pronounced them good.

Lord, how thy wonders are displayed

Where'er I turn my eye.

If I survey the ground I tread

Or gaze upon the sky!

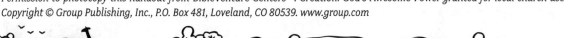

He's Got the Whole World in His Hands

He's got the whole world in his hands.

He's got the whole world in his hands.

He's got the whole world in his hands.

He's got the whole world in his hands.

He's got you and me brother in his hands.

He's got you and me brother in his hands.

He's got you and me brother in his hands.

He's got the whole world in his hands.

He's got you and me sister in his hands.

He's got you and me sister in his hands.

He's got you and me sister in his hands.

He's got the whole world in his hands.

He's got everybody here in his hands.

He's got everybody here in his hands.

He's got everybody here in his hands.

He's got the whole world in his hands.

What a Mighty God We Serve

What a mighty God we serve!

What a mighty God we serve!

Angels bow before him,

Heaven and earth adore him;

What a mighty God we serve.

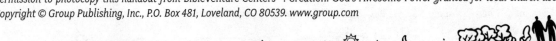

Job Description: BibleVenture Buddy

BibleVenture Buddies have the joy—and the challenge—of connecting with kids in a deep, significant way.

As a BibleVenture Buddy, here's what you'll become to the kids in your care...

A trusted friend. You're a grown-up who's glad these kids came, who knows their names, who's been praying about what's important to them. Your focused attention and listening ear help your kids realize they're important to you—and to God.

A role model. How you interact with kids sets the tone for how they'll interact with each other.

A guide. Instead of being the "teacher" with all the answers, you're someone who asks great questions. You jump in and enthusiastically do the activities *they* do at BibleVenture. You gently guide kids as they discover how to apply God's Word to their lives and enter into a deeper relationship with Jesus.

A steady influence in kids' lives. From week to week, you're there with a smile and kind word. You don't demand that kids perform to earn your approval. You don't give kids grades. You're in their corner, dependably cheering them on.

And as you serve God and the kids in your Venture Team, you'll help Jesus touch kids' hearts and change their lives—forever.

To be a spectacularly successful BibleVenture Buddy, it helps if you...
- love God,
- enjoy being with children,
- can be reflective and thoughtful,
- are comfortable talking with children about Jesus,
- believe children can understand and live God's Word,
- are accepting and supportive of children,
- model God's love in what you say and do, and
- like to laugh and have fun.

Responsibilities

As a BibleVenture Buddy, your responsibilities include...
- attending any scheduled training sessions,
- greeting children as they arrive,
- accompanying your Venture Team when traveling to a Center,
- joining in activities with your Venture Team,
- encouraging the kids in your Venture Team,
- facilitating discussions with your Venture Team,
- actively seeking to grow spiritually and in your leadership skills,
- assisting Center Leaders as needed,
- overseeing the sign-out sheet for your Venture Team, and
- praying for the children you serve.

Job Description: BibleVenture Center Leader

BibleVenture Center Leaders provide fun, engaging experiences for small groups of kids. Because the focus of each Center is slightly different, the skills required to lead each Center change from Center to Center, too.

But there are a few things *every* effective and successful Center Leader has in common. Successful Center Leaders...

- love God,
- enjoy and value children,
- are energetic and upbeat,
- maintain a positive attitude,
- can organize and motivate children to listen,
- are humble,
- are observant,
- attend scheduled leader training,
- prepare lessons thoroughly and with excellence, and
- model God's love in what they say and do.

At the BibleVenture Center program, Leaders serve in these two areas:

1. The Depot

The Depot Leader is the "up front" leader, helping kids transition into BibleVenture by leading a brief, fun, upbeat program.

You're responsible for...

- collecting necessary supplies,
- preparing and leading the weekly openings and closings with excellence,
- reinforcing the daily Bible Point as you lead,
- leading music, or finding someone to help you do so, and
- praying for the children and BibleVenture Buddies you serve.

2. Venture Centers

Venture Center Leaders encourage kids to form a lasting relationship with their BibleVenture Buddies, team members, and Jesus by leading an excellent 40-minute lesson.

You're responsible for...

- collecting necessary supplies,
- preparing and leading the weekly program with excellence,
- reinforcing the daily Bible Point as you lead,
- asking questions that will be discussed among the small groups (not with you!),
- cleaning up your area after your lesson, and
- praying for the children and volunteers in your BibleVenture program.

Job Description: BibleVenture Servant Leader

BibleVenture Servant Leaders support the BibleVenture program by jumping in to help where needed. You have a few assigned tasks but will probably do far more as you're asked to substitute for a missing BibleVenture Buddy, help out with a drama, gather supplies, or help out in another practical way.

Successful BibleVenture Servant Leaders...
- love God,
- enjoy and value children,
- are energetic and upbeat,
- maintain a positive attitude,
- are humble,
- are observant,
- attend scheduled leader training,
- have servant hearts, and
- model God's love in what they say and do.

Responsibilities
As a BibleVenture Servant Leader, your responsibilities include...
- attending any scheduled training sessions,
- greeting children as they arrive,
- staffing the Depot ticket window during the opening and closing times,
- encouraging kids and leaders,
- actively seeking to grow spiritually and in your leadership skills,
- assisting Center Leaders as needed, and
- praying for the children and leaders in your BibleVenture program.

BibleVenture Sign-In and Sign-Out Sheet

We value the children trusted to our care! Please sign your child in and out. And if there are people who are not permitted to pick up your child, please provide that information to our staff.

CHILD'S NAME:	PERSON SIGNING CHILD IN:	PERSON SIGNING CHILD OUT:	Check if ONLY the person signing child in can sign child out.

Bonus Training Session!

How to Introduce a Child to Jesus

Use this training session to help your leaders discover how to encourage a child to form a relationship with Jesus.

Please note that you may choose to adapt this session; it doesn't take into consideration all the nuances that vary from denomination to denomination. Instead, it communicates those Bible truths that are consistent across most denominations.

Supplies
- Bibles (one per pair of leaders)
- name tags
- train whistle or other attention-getting noisemaker
- chairs
- CD or tape player
- newsprint and a marker
- snacks

Getting Ready

Before the meeting, set the CD player where everyone will be able to easily hear it. In the back of the room, set up a table for snack supplies.

Set out name tags where leaders will be able to find the tags as they enter the room.

Play relaxing music as leaders enter.

Getting Started

When you're ready to begin, gradually turn down the volume of the music, then stop the CD. Blow your train whistle or use another attention-getting signal. Thank everyone for coming and for helping with the BibleVenture program.

Take a few minutes to discuss how your program is going and what suggestions people have to improve it. However, be careful this discussion doesn't consume your training time.

Introducing a child to Jesus is extremely important—it has eternal impact!

Before leading this training, talk with your pastor or children's director to make sure you have an accurate understanding of what steps and methods your church approves. You may even want one of your church leaders to sit in, as a "guest authority," during this training. You *don't* want to find out after the training that what you taught somehow violates your church's procedures. Ask about parental involvement, doctrine, and age of children.

If you discover serious issues that need to be resolved, set up another time to meet with the people involved.

SAY **We're all here because we're involved in God's work of helping kids grow closer to God, each other, and significant, caring adults. Each of you is a valuable part of our BibleVenture staff. Let's start our training time with prayer.**

PRAY **Dear God, thank you for each person—each leader—here. We all want to help children find you and grow in their faith. Guide us as we explore ways to help kids connect with you, and help us find ways that we can lead them to develop a lifelong relationship with you. In Jesus' name, amen.**

Have leaders form trios. Once leaders are in trios, SAY **Isn't it amazing how you can work with people and not know some of the important things in their lives?**

Today, we'll get a little closer to one another by sharing the answers to four simple questions. The person who has most recently eaten a candy bar will begin.

Read the following questions one at a time. Pause after each question and allow your staff to answer the questions and discuss the implications.

1. What is your favorite dessert?

2. Describe one of the top five days of your life.

3. What was the name of your first pet, and what sort of pet was it?

4. What were the circumstances around your inviting Jesus Christ into your life?

Once trios have had a chance to struggle with the last question for a few moments, blow the train whistle.

ASK

● **Why is it so easy to tell someone about your favorite dessert or the best day of your life, yet more difficult to describe why and how you came to enter into a relationship with Jesus Christ?**

Allow leaders to suggest answers.

SAY **Let's change our activity a bit. Stay in your same groups, but in each trio, two of you need to sit back-to-back. The only requirement is that one of you who's sitting back-to-back has to be wearing shoes that lace up and tie.**

After everyone is in place, SAY **Person wearing shoes that tie, untie your shoes. Got them untied? Good. Now you'll tie them again, but let's pretend you don't know how. Your partner will tell you how to do the task, but you may *only* do what your partner tells you to do; no more, no less.**

Those of you sitting back-to-back with a partner who's just untied his or her shoes, you'll give step-by-step directions for tying shoes. Piece of cake, right? You've done it a million times yourself.

The third person in each trio is the NATO (Never A Tying Obstacle) Observer. Your job is to make sure the step-by-step instructions are carried out word for word; no more, no less. And you'll be on hand if a thumb is caught in a knot and needs medical attention.

Remember: Give detailed, step-by-step instructions. You must assume that the person tying the shoe has never seen a shoe before and has no *idea* how to tie a knot.

Begin now. You've got four minutes to complete the assignment.

Encourage trios as they attempt this frustrating task. Give two-minute and one-minute warnings. When time has elapsed, bring trios together in a large group.

ASK

● **Why was it hard to give instructions when you couldn't see how they were being received or followed?**

● **How difficult was it to understand instructions? Why? Please give an example.**

● **How is this activity like or unlike leading a child to Christ?**

Keep a record of answers on a piece of newsprint.

SAY **At BibleVenture we want to help children grow closer to Jesus. For non-Christian kids, that means introducing them to Jesus and inviting those children to enter into a relationship with him. If we're unprepared to share what a relationship with Jesus is, or how to enter into one, we may confuse kids rather than help them grow closer to Jesus.**

Every week at BibleVenture there's a distinct possibility that we'll enter into a conversation with a child about Jesus. But are we comfortable answering their questions about Jesus in a kid-friendly way? In the next few minutes, let's practice the skills we need to share our faith in Jesus with a child.

If some of your trios don't include people who have shoes that tie, rearrange the trio memberships.

Know Your Own Faith Story

SAY **We all have a faith story, but that doesn't mean we've thought it through enough to share it with others. Here's a quick test to see if you're ready to share your faith story. Don't answer these questions right now, but do consider: How would you answer if you were asked?**

- **When did you become a Christian?**

- **What difference does being a Christian make in your daily life?**

- **What has God done in your life?**

- **What is God doing now in your life?**

- **Can you include Scriptures to bring biblical authority to your story?**

- **Can you relate the entire experience in two minutes or less?**

And here's a question that gets at why we might want to share our faith story in the first place:

- **Why would you want a child to know Jesus?**

SAY **Now, I know that many people consider their faith stories a deeply personal matter. They don't want to "inflict" their faith stories on others. They don't want to be thought intolerant or rude.**

Other people are hesitant to share their faith stories because they fear the conversation will prompt questions they can't answer. For instance, what if someone on the other end of a faith story raises an eyebrow and says, "Yeah? Well, what about creation? Were those *literal* days?" Or there's a question about Scripture, church history, doctrine, hermeneutics, transubstantiation, or the Second Coming. What then?

So these Christians fly along below the radar, not identifying themselves and not sharing what they know to be true: their own story.

There's a critical difference between launching into a lecture proving the validity of the resurrection and sharing what's happened to you.

And *that's* your faith story: what's happened to you. No more, and no less. It's great to know Scripture and to understand deeply all the issues surrounding theology and church history. But that information is secondary to your faith story.

Ask leaders to stand, and tell them they're about to be in an instant drama. The good news: There are no lines to memorize, no need to burst into song, no need to worry about reviews in the morning paper.

Also: There's no audience. *Everyone* is a participant.

Ask for volunteers to fill the following roles: Jesus, a blind man, disciples, Pharisees (three or four people), and neighbors. Once you have those roles filled, position people in the "stage area" (anywhere without chairs to trip over!), with the Pharisees and neighbors on one side of the stage, Jesus and the disciples in the middle, and the blind man at the far end of the stage.

By the way, if you have just a few leaders at your training, cast Jesus, the blind man, and one Pharisee...and *you* can play the role of the Pharisee! Toss in a neighbor if one's available.

Tell your actors to act along with the cues they'll hear in the following fun version of John chapter 9. Read it aloud, and encourage actors to get into their roles.

The Blind Man's Faith Story

As Jesus walked along, he saw a man who had been blind from birth. The blind man was sitting on the ground, begging for money.

Jesus' disciples saw the blind man, too, and pointed the man out. Then the disciples turned to Jesus.

"Teacher, who sinned, this man or his parents?"

The disciples thought the man was born blind because someone had done something wrong. The disciples thought this was a very deep question. See how they scratch their chins and look like they're thinking deep thoughts? Now see them give each other high fives, celebrating that they asked such a profound question?

Jesus turned to the disciples.

"Neither this man nor his parents sinned," said Jesus. Jesus pointed to the man's eyes. "This happened so that the work of God might be displayed in this man's life."

The disciples looked confused. They looked at one another and scratched their heads.

Jesus sighed a big sigh and continued talking, gesturing as he talked. "As long as it is day, we must do the work of him who sent me. Night is coming, when no one can work. While I am in the world, I am the light of the world."

Jesus then knelt next to the blind man. Jesus spit—hey, we're just *acting* here!—on the ground and made some mud by pushing the dirt and spit around with his index finger.

95

Then Jesus took the mud and put some on the left eye of the blind man. Then he put mud on the right eye of the blind man.

Then Jesus stood up and helped the blind man stand up.

Jesus told the blind man to go to the Pool of Siloam to wash.

The blind man did this. First he washed his face to get the mud off. Then he washed his hair. Then he washed behind his ears. Then he stopped and rubbed his eyes because something was wrong. Instead of seeing the comfortable black he'd known his whole life, he could see things.

He stared at his hands.

Then he stared at his feet (he'd never seen feet before).

Then he stared at other people's feet.

Then he went back home, and he greeted his neighbors.

The neighbors were amazed. They could tell the man could see, which meant they'd have to start calling him something besides The Blind Man. They put their heads together in a huddle to talk about this, and after taking a vote, they decided to call him Larry.

Some of the neighbors knew that Larry was the man who had been blind from birth. Some of the neighbors couldn't believe a blind man would be able to see again, so they said maybe Larry just *looked* like the blind man.

But Larry nodded his head and said, "I'm the same guy."

So the neighbors asked, "Then what happened? How did your eyes start working?"

Larry pointed back at where he'd been healed. He was excited as he told what had happened. "Well, I was sitting on the ground begging, just like this," Larry said. "Then the man they call Jesus made some mud and put it on my eyes, like this. Then I went to Siloam and washed, like this. Then I could see—like this!"

The neighbors looked around. They looked up...then down...then to the left...then to the right. "Where is this Jesus?" they asked.

Larry shrugged. "I dunno," he said.

The neighbors grabbed Larry by the elbows and took him to see the Pharisees.

The Pharisees were important religious men. They stood tall and proud. They stroked their beards. They didn't smile because they were busy being important and right. Being right was really important to the Pharisees, and after they heard about Larry they knew something wasn't right.

The Pharisees held up a hand to tell the neighbors to quiet down. The Pharisees pointed to Larry and asked Larry to tell what happened.

Larry quickly showed them. First, he'd been sitting on the ground, begging. Then Jesus put mud on his eyes. Then Larry got up and went to the pool and washed. Then he could see.

The tallest of the Pharisees looked thoughtful. He asked Larry to explain again, so Larry did.

First, on the ground. Then mud in the eye. Then to the pool to wash. Then he could see.

The tallest Pharisee lifted an index finger in a meaningful way. He nodded to the other Pharisees and the neighbors. The healing had happened on the *Sabbath*.

All the neighbors and Pharisees shook their heads sadly. Doing work on the Sabbath was a sin, so Jesus couldn't be working for God.

Some Pharisees turned to the left. They decided that Jesus must not be from God because he worked on the Sabbath.

Other Pharisees turned to the right. They thought Jesus must be from God because no sinner could do miracles.

Finally, all the Pharisees turned to Larry. They pointed at Larry again and said, "What have *you* to say about him? It was *your* eyes he opened."

Larry said, "I think Jesus is a prophet."

The Pharisees looked angry. They stamped their feet and squinted with fury.

The Pharisees pointed at Larry and said, "We know Jesus must be a sinner."

Larry shrugged. He said, "I don't know if he's a sinner or not, but I know this: I was blind but now I can see."

The Pharisees didn't want to hear that. They scrunched up their faces in fury again. They stamped their feet even harder. They tore out their hair.

The Pharisees shook their fingers at Larry. "What did he *do* to you? How did he open your eyes?"

Larry shrugged again and said, "I already told you and you didn't listen. Why do you want to hear it again? Do you want to become his disciples too?"

The Pharisees were so angry they shook. Then two of them took Larry's elbows. They aimed him toward the door. The tallest Pharisee said, "You were steeped in sin at birth; how dare you lecture us!"

And the Pharisees threw Larry out.

Applaud your actors, then SAY **Before you sit down again, form pairs with someone you haven't been in a group with yet today.**

Ask pairs to discuss:

● **How would you summarize the blind man's faith story in a sentence or two?**

● **How effectively did the blind man share his faith story?**

● **Jesus healed the blind man's eyes. If you were asked what Jesus has done for you, how would you answer?**

After pairs have had several minutes to talk, call their attention back to you using your attention-getting signal.

SAY **One reason I'm glad this incident is included in Scripture is that while the blind man knew almost nothing about Jesus, he stated what Jesus had done simply and clearly.**

And nobody could contest the man's experience.

Our faith stories are most powerful when they're based on our own experiences, when they're first-person testimonies rather than reports of what others have said.

Plus, it's *our* stories that children want to hear. They want to know what's real and immediate, what we know to be true—not what we think might be true.

Let's spend some time discovering our faith stories. They probably won't be as dramatic as what happened to the blind man, but that's OK!

In your pairs, let's briefly answer those questions I asked earlier. You'll have about two minutes to discuss each question.

ASK

● **When did you become a Christian?**

● **What difference does being a Christian make in your daily life?**

● **What has God done in your life?**

● **What is God doing now in your life?**

- **Can you include Scriptures to bring biblical authority to your story?**

- **Can you relate the entire experience in two minutes or less?**

- **Why would you want a child to know Jesus?**

SAY **Kids don't want or need to know a lot of theology. They want to know if Jesus is real, and if so, what difference Jesus makes in your life. *That's* your story. The theology will come later as kids grow in their faith. But to begin, we need to simply introduce kids to Jesus. Here are six things to keep in mind as you introduce a child to Christ.**

1. Discover what *category* of child you're talking with.

SAY **Kids come to our BibleVenture program from three places: our church, other churches, and from unchurched families. And all three require slightly different considerations when you're sharing Jesus with them. Consider...**

- **When sharing about Jesus with kids from our church, do so according to our policies and in alignment with our traditions.**

Note: Provide this information rather than assuming your adults all understand it. Having a church leader briefly explain what children's workers need to know would probably be appropriate here, if you think it's needed.

- **When sharing Christ with kids from *other* churches, encourage kids to follow up by talking with their own pastors.**

SAY **Why? Because unless a child's family transfers to our church, we won't be the ones providing long-term, church-based Christian education. Encouraging kids to bring their own pastors into the loop isn't just a professional courtesy; it's for the good of the child.**

That *doesn't* mean you should refuse to introduce children from other churches to Jesus! Instead, share and then find out who at the child's home church needs to hear about the discussion.

Note: If you're the director of your BibleVenture, you might be the most appropriate person to serve as a liaison for this sort of discussion. If that's the case, let your leaders know.

ASK

- **If children have *no* church background, ask lots of questions.**

SAY **Be sure children can explain what they've heard in their own words. Find out what kind of faith support the child will have at home. Remember: For better or worse, parents are the primary faith shapers of their children.**

Note: As the director of your BibleVenture program, what are your strategies for communicating with parents and supporting them as faith shapers? Briefly share those strategies with your team.

2. Ask questions—don't assume.

SAY **When children ask about coming to Christ, don't assume they're ready to make that decision at that precise moment. Children may just be curious. Probe with questions to determine how much they understand. Here are two good questions...**

● **Who is Jesus, and what important thing did he do?** If the child doesn't know who Jesus is and that he died to save us from our sins, this is a good place to begin explaining.

● **Have you ever sinned?** If children say "no," their understanding of what Jesus saved them from is incomplete. If they say "yes," ask for a nonthreatening example to use as an example in further discussion.

3. Be careful of using "church lingo."

SAY **Words like *repent, confession,* and *conversion* aren't widely used in normal conversation or age appropriate for young children. If you use these words, give a brief explanation or illustration each time you do.**

Ask yourself, "Would *I* understand what I'm saying if I were this child's age?"

4. Point to relevant Scriptures.

SAY **Jesus wants a friendship with your children, and there are benefits of having that friendship. Help kids realize those truths by showing them Bible passages where that invitation is given.**

Ask leaders to form pairs and be sure each pair has a Bible. Have them look up the following verses and read them aloud: John 3:16; Romans 5:8-11; Romans 6:23; and Ephesians 2:4-9.

SAY **These are great passages to commit to memory so you're always "prepared to give an answer to everyone who asks you to give the reason for the hope that you have" (1 Peter 3:15).**

If you don't want to memorize them, know where to find them so you can open up your Bible and show a child that God wants him or her as a forever friend.

5. Bring parents in on the discussion.

SAY **Our BibleVenture program and children's parents are a team. Ask children's permission to bring their parents into the discussion. Some kids will feel better if their parents are involved in the whole discussion, and others will prefer to talk without their parents in the room.**

Either way, make certain parents know about spiritual decisions made by their children.

6. Don't be afraid to ask for help.

SAY **Spiritual discussions can quickly become complex. If you feel you're in over your head, ask the child if you can bring in a friend to help you answer questions. Then turn to someone you trust.**

Explain clearly who's available to provide help, and if possible introduce those people.

Ask if any of the leaders have stories to share that illustrate any of these points. Be prepared to monitor this discussion carefully; stories can become long and complicated. Be sensitive about the time.

Wrapping Up

Ask leaders if they have any questions. Invite experienced leaders to add suggestions to what you've been discussing. When you have about 15 minutes left, move to the next activity.

SAY **Let's make sure we're ready the next time we're given the chance to introduce a child to Jesus. Form pairs and let's take turns sharing our faith stories with each other.**

This is the chance to help another leader sharpen his or her faith story so it's easily understood by a child. With that in mind—the desire to be helpful, not critical—offer constructive suggestions to each other.

Be sure that you share your story in a way that

● **is directed to the category of child you're talking to (churched, other churched, unchurched). How do you know? Ask.**

● **honors the child's spiritual life. Does the child already know Jesus as a friend? Is the child seeking? Is the child simply curious? Again—ask.**

● **is age appropriate, without complicated words or "churchy" language.**

● **includes brief, relevant Scriptures. I'll give you a copy of the ones I mentioned earlier.** Distribute handouts, one to each leader.

If you get stuck or need help, let me know and I'll do what I can to be of help.

We'll each have five minutes to share our faith story and lead our partners through the Bible passages. I'll let you know when four minutes have passed for each presentation.

Walk among the pairs to keep them on task. Offer advice where necessary, but let leaders deal with issues on their own terms. Their faith stories need to be precisely that...*their* faith stories.

When you have about five minutes left before dismissing, ask leaders to join hands and pray. Together ask God to provide opportunities to introduce children to Jesus.

Invite leaders to stick around for a few minutes to share a snack. Leaders in children's ministry want to feel connected—to each other, and to you. That can happen wonderfully during an unstructured goodie time!

Creation—God's Awesome Power

BibleVenture Invitation Letter

Dear Brian,

Stars exploding into light and spinning across the universe...thundering herds of animals stampeding across a grassy plain...a perfect garden where a tempting tree is heavy with forbidden fruit...

Sounds like a Hollywood movie, doesn't it?

Except this isn't a movie...it's true! And you can learn all about it!

You're invited to join us at *BibleVenture™: Creation—God's Awesome Power* each Sunday night starting July 6th at 6:00 p.m.

We'll meet for four Sundays in a row—all July—and you won't want to miss a single night!

Each one-hour program will have you visiting different BibleVenture Centers. One week you may be acting in a fun, no-lines-to-learn drama presentation. Another week you may be crafting an art project to take home. There's always something different, and it's always fun!

Tell your mom or dad right now that you want to join your friends at BibleVenture on July 6th! Circle the date on the family calendar! That's the date the adventure begins...and who knows where it will end?

It just might change your life!

Sincerely,

Audrey Ferris
BibleVenture Director,
First Church
555-1212

Invite kids to your BibleVentures™: Creation—God's Awesome Power program! Adapt this invitation to fit your schedule and church letterhead, then send a copy to each child in your Sunday school. Post copies on community bulletin boards, and send invitations to neighborhood children who visited your vacation Bible School, too!

Leader Encouragement Pages

Can you imagine doing a BibleVenture program without volunteer leaders? It wouldn't happen!

So thank your leaders weekly with these reproducible pages. You've got one page for each week of this BibleVenture program.

Each week, make a copy of one page for each of your leaders. Slip copies into envelopes, and send each volunteer an encouraging letter. Make it even more special by jotting a personal note on each copy you send.

The volunteer experts at Group's Church Volunteer Central (www.churchvolunteercentral.com) report that a leading reason volunteers resign their positions is that they don't feel recognized and appreciated.

You can help your precious children's ministry leaders feel valued by saying "thanks!" on a regular basis...and these pages will help!

You're the Best!

For God so loved the world that he gave his one and only Son, that whoever believes in him shall not perish but have eternal life.

—John 3:16

What an important message you're sharing with children!

Thanks for your faithfulness in not just telling kids this truth, but living it out in front of children, too. Your life is a testimony that points children to Jesus!

But because of his great love for us, God, who is rich in mercy, made us alive with Christ even when we were dead in transgressions—it is by grace you have been saved. And God raised us up with Christ and seated us with him in the heavenly realms in Christ Jesus, in order that in the coming ages he might show the incomparable riches of his grace, expressed in his kindness to us in Christ Jesus. For it is by grace you have been saved, through faith—and this not from yourselves, it is the gift of God—not by works, so that no one can boast.

—Ephesians 2:4-9

It's God's love that saves us...and the kids we serve. Thank you for "being alive with Christ" and letting him use you.

The ministry you have with children is changing the world!

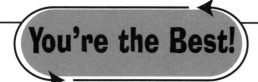

You're the Best!

"Carry each other's burdens, and in this way you will fulfill the law of Christ."

—Galatians 6:2

Let's be there for each other. How can you encourage another adult who serves at our BibleVenture program?

You're the Best!

"Great is the Lord and most worthy of praise; his greatness no one can fathom. One generation will commend your works to another; they will tell of your mighty acts. They will speak of the glorious splendor of your majesty, and I will meditate on your wonderful works. They will tell of the power of your awesome works, and I will proclaim your great deeds."

—Psalm 145:3-6

From generation to generation, God's praises and mighty works have been made known. As you teach children about their Creator, you're part of that chain of praise! Thank you for all you do!

How to Connect With Kids

Dear BibleVenture Leader,

For just a moment, think about your favorite teacher in grade school.

Can you remember that person? Picture the teacher's face and—if you can—the classroom where you spent time with that teacher. Fix that face and space in your mind.

Now think about *why* that teacher was your favorite.

I'm willing to bet it wasn't because the teacher was especially good at providing instruction about geography or at teaching the alphabet. While your favorite teacher might have sparkled at his or her teaching skills, it's not likely that's why you connected in such a meaningful way.

Rather, I'm willing to bet that you connected with that teacher *personally*. You had a *relationship* with him or her, and it's that relationship you remember so warmly.

Here's what you probably *don't* remember: Your favorite teacher probably did lots of little things to connect with you, to communicate warmth and caring. Maybe it was tucking a valentine card in your box, or remembering your birthday. Maybe it was simply knowing your name when so many adults didn't bother to learn it.

Whatever those little things were, it's likely that no matter how special they made you feel, the teacher did the same things with other students too.

That's right: *Your* favorite teacher is probably other people's favorite teacher! The little habits and connection skills used with you probably endeared your teacher to other kids too.

It's the little things that count—and connect

Now think about your role in our BibleVenture program. You have contact with kids week after week, and that means you have the potential to be the teacher someone remembers fondly 20 years from now when picturing a face from the past.

That's right—*you* can be that children's leader who has such a huge impact on a child that you're remembered long after the child has become an adult.

To do that you'll need to do your job well at BibleVenture, but you'll need to do something more.

You'll need to connect with kids.

How to Connect With Kids

I want to suggest three "little things" that will go a long way toward connecting you with kids. They're habits you can easily develop, and they'll cost you nothing...but will give kids a bridge into a relationship with you.

1. Be approachable.

Ever talk with someone standing on a stepladder or on steps? Uncomfortable, isn't it?

That's what it's like for children to talk with adults—especially tall ones. Kids crane their necks, and strain to hear what grown-ups are saying. And then there's the other challenge: what to call you.

Here are some easy ways to be approachable to children...

● **Kneel when you're talking with kids.** This removes the obstacle of your height difference, and let's you engage children in eye-to-eye conversation.

● **Be cheerful—and smile.** When adults appear grumpy or angry, children often wonder if it's their fault. So be deliberate about leaving your disgust with the crack in your car windshield out in the parking lot with your car. When you enter the room for BibleVenture, be smiling and welcoming.

● **Wear a name tag.** Not only does this help children remember your name, but it signals how you want to be addressed. If you write "Mrs. Smith," that's what kids will call you. But if you write "Sally," that gives children permission to call you by your first name.

● **Use children's names in conversations.** If your memory is wired so names escape you, go to the trouble of having kids wear name tags. Or simply make it important enough to learn names.

● **Wear comfortable clothing that lets you enter into activities.** In any given BibleVenture program, your kids might be painting, skipping, or pretending they're in an earthquake as they roll around on the floor. Be dressed so you can join them!

2. Share your life—within reason.

Grown-ups lead lives that are completely different from lives lived by children. It's like we're on different planets. That's why it's critical that, in a healthy way, you share what's happening in your life.

Because kids aren't your peers, you need to be careful about what you share. Never make a child uncomfortable or responsible for more information than he or she can bear.

How to Connect With Kids

That still leaves plenty of material that's appropriate to discuss. Your family, for instance, or upcoming travel plans. General health issues might be appropriate, too, and work- or school-related topics.

Here are several simple ways to share your life with your children...

● **When it's prayer time, share something.** Asking children to pray for you and your life communicates that you value both prayer and your kids.

● **Bring in a picture of your family to pass around.** Maybe it's your husband and kids, or your parents, or even a candid picture of your dog (do they take formal dog photos?). It doesn't matter what the photo is; the fact you're passing it around gives children a sense that you live in the real world. You're not just the person they see at church.

3. Have fun.

The children's version of that famous saying reads this way: "The families that play together, stay together."

At our BibleVenture we're trying to build a family atmosphere. That's why children are in small groups, with consistent adult leadership. That's why we encourage relationship building.

And what do they call the person in a family who never enters into games or parties? A *party pooper*, that's what!

Don't be a party pooper. Dive in to activities with your kids as your playmates. Your participation gives you a shared experience with the kids and provides a richer, more authentic debriefing time after visiting Venture Centers.

Here are some ways to have fun with children...

● **Check your dignity at the door.** OK, maybe you don't particularly want to stick your hands in paint and leave a handprint on a banner. So what? Do it anyway, and enter into the spirit of the moment alongside your kids. Sing along even if you don't sing well. Play the game even if you know you won't win. Play a part in the drama even if you know there's no Academy Award in your future.

● **Participate in everything.** That means the snack (if you serve one), the skits, the games...everything. If you give yourself permission to opt out of some activities, your kids will do the same. Your participation sets the standard—make sure that standard is "we do it all." If you're not participating, there's no chance for you to have fun with your kids!

How to Connect With Kids

● **Don't be competitive.** If you feel you should make a good showing because you're the grown-up, get over it. Relax and enjoy yourself, and consider it all joy should a child beat you across the finish line in the toe-to-heel relay.

After all, is winning that race really so important for your career advancement? A high score for you means nothing; to a child it's what makes a great day.

How hard is it to connect with kids in a significant, life-changing way?

It takes a decision that kids are important, and your volunteering to serve at BibleVenture shows you've already decided that.

It takes a childlike (not *childish*) heart and willingness to let others in.

And it takes placing good connection habits into your daily life and ministry. You can start with those identified above, but they're just the tip of the iceberg. Watch adults who kids love and you'll find more and more behaviors that tear down barriers and build bridges instead. Plug those behaviors into your own ministry style; you'll see kids warm up to you even more.

God bless you as you serve kids. You're doing work that will change lives—the lives of your kids and your own life too!

Make a copy of this letter for each of your BibleVenture volunteers!